Gemini

By Creshie Writes

Gemini©

Copyright © 2017 by Creshie Writes

Printed in USA by Create space
Artwork drawn by Creshie Writes
Head shot photo by Quamell Espada, IG@qmilly
Cover graphic design layout by the amazing Patrick

Thank yous...

First and foremost praises to my higher power, which gives me life. To my children for keeping me young, to my grandson "Pickle" who is a daily reminder what LIVING is really all about, to my soldiers, Dr. Olivia Ghaw and Whoopi Goldberg, they stand by my side with words of encouragement, love and wisdom, through my daily war against Lupus, also giving a thank to my dear friend Eric Estrada for teaching me the power of healing through food, the fuel to my writing comes from my chapter by chapter readers, Day, Devera,Tia, Tiffany, Monica, Milton, and Honora, either I'm harassing them to read or they are pushing me for a new chapter. And last but not least THANK YOU! To each and every set of hands who pick up any of my book. I write for you!

XOXO

It was the beginning of the spring but felt cold as winter, standing on top of the damp grass, under the stars in the sky and the sound of a seashell humming in my ear from the trees swaying against the night's breeze. Stray pieces of my hair flew away from my bun that rested on the back of my head was dancing in the air's light draft. I use my fingers to clear the strings of hair from my sight. The leaves rustling on the ground is daunting like Mother Nature was giving me a sign that something was about to happen. A chill crept up my shine, made my stomach turn flips and caused the palm of my hands to start sweating. I felt weak and sick. I just wanted to go home but I was too afraid to leave and miss the events to come. I also was scared to death to stay. Mimi hovered over me like she was addicted to the smell of fear oozing off me. We stood face to face I could literally feel every word she said.

"I know you're scared, we all are but we have to do this to protect our secret."

"But to what lengths are we willing to go to preserve the secret?"

I wish I could snatch the question out the air and swallow my words. Mimi whole face change from the sweetest, loving, caring person I've ever met to an unrecognizable angry, evil being with a slightly demonic contoured face. I stood face to face with a sweet dream and vicious nightmare. I was so petrified I started crying it was the only bodily function I could control. It was like my tongue was stuck to the roof of my mouth preventing me from talking. My feet felt too heavy for my legs like my Gucci loaves was filled with cement and I can't walk. I had the sensation of being in a coma. I could see and hear everything going on around me but I couldn't respond. It's all too overwhelming. Mimi had convinced Tricia that Nicole was talking to Lippa's police officer uncle about our illegal hustle. The ins and outs to our excessive life style in the hand on NYPD would grantee a long stay behind bars. Tricia found high fashion to fit each one of our personality. Adults, parents and teachers envied the way we dress and lived. We all wore the top of the line clothes, shoes, trinkets and purses, we also eat at the top restaurants, which made our peers our enemies. Mimi assured me, we all would be arrested and forced to do time in prison for the black box hustle alone. I would never call Mimi a liar but I didn't believe Nicole would tell. Not only because she was actually a key component to the scam but cause she's addicted to retail just like Tricia. They would never jeopardized fashion for jail. But the threat to Tricia's wardrobe was enough to push her into savage mood. Mimi had taken Tricia on long guilt trip for acquainting Erica and Nicole into our inner circle. Especially since the introduction back fired in the worst way. The built guilty conscious in Tricia made her willing to travel to new lows to correct an unintentional error. Mimi had transformed the bubbly fashionista into a shaken soda, fizzing ready to pop. The sight of this side of Tricia gave me goose bumps up the sides of my face. Seeing the distorted Tricia alarmed every sense in my bones. I'm literally shaking in the breeze feeling uneasy inside and out. Free is usually the diplomat. The ambassador of unity and love. Free's natural calmness is the quality she is best known for. She comfort sensitive politic injustice in a monotone manner. But Mimi created a fidgety loudmouth with evil red eyes, named Free. The vision of the unnatural Free made my heart beat fast and the hairs on the back of my neck stand up. Mimi manipulated Free's picture perfect secret relationship to display something shameful. Free's perception of being with Erica changed from being something special to being a public spectacle. Free harbored over the thought of Erica spreading details about their lesbian affair. Thoughts planted by Mimi's cruel words. Mimi feed, nurtured, and raised the bad seeds of deceit in Free's head. Threaten exposure stole the civil Free from existence. Mimi had twisted Free and Tricia's vision. They started hallucinating viewing everyday behavior as suspicious evidences toward Mimi's words. Mimi's daily relentless words of Erica's and Nicole's betrayal provoked Free and Tricia to boil with rage. Mimi knew what to say to trigger emotion in each one of us. Mimi has pushed us way pass our limits. Going past my limit was scary enough but not being able to turn back made tears stream down my face. We all feared Mimi as much as we feared life without her. Mimi had the ultimate plan to gives us all freedom from our past and independence to our futures. Oh and most importantly we would escape possible jail time. We motivated and annoyed each other equally. With tears wetting my cold rosy cheeks and fly away hairs sticking to my wet face I stood still looking through Mimi. On no occasion would I ever disagree with Mimi even if I was right. Yes I was book smart, Free is hands down number one when it comes to the real black history and nobody could ever be on top of fashion more than Tricia but Mimi knew tricks to all trades. My brain was telling my heart Mimi knows best but my heart wasn't feeling it. Silently I totally disagree with the whole plan. Every trivial crime we have ever committed thus far, nobody ever got hurt. I could feel it in my bones this night was going to be the breaking point off our teenage years and we were going to wake up in the morning adults with a scar that will never heal. Yet I said nothing instead I cried til my body shivered. My body language infuriated Mimi. She used her right hand to grab me by my face. The demonic look in her eyes paralyzed me. She started talking thru her teeth but her lips were moving. Tears roll out the corner of my eyes because my eyelids refuse to blink. Mimi had turned into a product of the environment, dark, creepy and cold.

"You better stop that fucking crying, NOW! Can you handle being in a padded white room alone again? You know you're going there alone, right? They wouldn't allow any of us to come visit you, you remember? It's been that long? You forgot? Being alone and cold, sing yourself to sleep with your own cries. Or being so drugged up to dope fiend status, drooling and nodding in a corner while the orderlies plot on your belongings public or personal? Feeling so low can't even pick yourself up to take a shower. Smelling like a bag of onions cause you rotten from the inside out. Do you have the strength to make it thru that again? Or, are you going to be weak and go back to the ward? I need a fucking answer right fucking now?"

A flood of tears roll down my cheek as my fly away hairs feel like tree sider's webs stuck to my face. Mimi words pierced my heart and I bleed with pure pain. How could she use my darkest moment as collateral damage? I seen Mimi sling words in the most pleasant manner slapping a heart with gentleness, I've also seen her toss words at ninety miles per hour with foul disgust, gut punching, bringing a person's dignity to its knees. But anytime she pitch her words in the air they land on manipulating any situations to her favor by verbally controlling people. As Mimi throw verbal jabs, upper cuts and body blows my mind had a mental flash back to the horror of the icy white walls under everlasting gray skies, the scent of redundant amounts of bleach on the floors in a failed attempt to covering blood, feces and urine. The frosty panic of being in complete isolation washed over the present me flushing color out my skin. The anxiety of returning to the past fueled my determination to secure my future. I had decided at that very moment after this last deed was done I was going to cut ties with Mimi not because she is a savage animal but because she had the ability to bring out the vicious savage animal in me. Her hand pressured my face for an answer by squeezing my cheeks in. Mimi is interrupted by Dom pulling up in Ms. Janet's run downed green '97 Honda

Civic with Erica, Free, Nicole and Tricia in the back seat. Even though Mimi wasn't in the car nobody dare sit in the front passage seat, I wasn't sure if it was out of fear or out of respect?

"Clean your face and pull your shit together or do Dom need to drop your ass off at the nut farm?"

I clean my face. I didn't want the others to see Mimi's work on my feelings. As Mimi continue to swing into my open wounds with her hurtful words.

"Yo, what's really good with you? I thought we was going to Calvin's party. I paid too much for this damn Channel leather jacket to be in the fucking woods." Nicole words questioned Mimi before she stepped out the car.

"Ah, shut up you used your employee discount." Free teased Nicole before her tongue dance with Erica's tongue.

"It still cost a lot. And I want everybody and their mother to see me in it!"

"Nicole calm down the fucking jacket is fire truck red ain't nobody going to miss you in it, you can bet on that, trust me. I can't wait to rock it my damn self!" Tricia joked.

"But, really why are we here?"

"To get a little buzz on before the party."

It wasn't unusual for Dom to chauffeur us out to our Brentwood camp ground. There wasn't another person within four miles from us in either direction. In the Long Island forest underage drinking and illegal weed smoked in the privacy of Mother Nature was permitted. Being out here basing in our slice of teenage freedom. Mimi took her seat, as if it was her throne and she was ready to rein. Dom is Mimi silent partner, lover, and her reinforcements. Dom never left the driver's seat. He turned up the music playing on the car radio. He sat next to Mimi like her king. Erica, Nicole, Free, and Tricia laid on the hood of the car looking up at the stars, flying on cloud nine. I stood on the sideline watching. My chest was still burning from Mimi's verbal assault. She washed my face with my frightening past memories that I confined in her. At that time my mother had just died and I was struggling with emotional upset. I was broken and was unable to find the pieces. I had to be institutionalized cause I was deemed a threat to myself and others. She brought it up and it pulled me down. While they were laughing at the good times, having a good time, I just stared at Mimi. Mimi was being extra nice, her evil was showing. With days away from finishing our senior year I was ready to move forward and leave them all in the past. We shared four years of friendship and a partnership in business. The bond has taught me plenty of life lessons that will stay with me for the rest of my life. But being close friends with Mimi came with the price of frightening memories, a constant sense of danger and feeling completely numb towards another person's emotional state. Mimi is very territorial over her friends. She build up a wall with thick bricks of lies making it impossible to get over and still have the ability to trust people. I observed the faces of the people I've co-existed with for the last four years and started wonder when did I disconnect from the rest of the world and will I be able to pick up and reconnect the human race once they are all gone? After a while the liquor started talking for them. Panic gave me a voice and I asked Dom to take us to party now. The stars had stop shinning and the sky was moonless. The murkiness of danger smoked at my feet.

"Tricia, its no hard feelings..."

"Hard feeling?"

"Yeah, no hard feeling, I know you still fucking Lippa..." Nicole tossed the words in the air for Tricia's feelings to catch. But Dom reached in and snagged the words from the air. He grab the words the wrong way and punched the back of Mimi's head rest. Mimi's head jerked forward from the blow. I didn't get why Dom would care about who Tricia is fucking or maybe it was the fact Tricia was fucking Lippa. Lippa is Dom brother without sharing DNA. Whatever it was it damn sure pissed him off and Dom angry is ten times worse than evil Mimi, if that's even possible.

"...but it's all good. I've been fucking his Uncle any way! Besides my mother always taught me to give my "USED" toys to the less fortunate. And oh yeah Mimi me and Erica is out your business, this hustle is crumbs for a bunch of birds. And you better play nice with your crazy ass or I'll have popo throw you ass in jail before you could think of another name."

Mimi caught the words that Nicole hurled in the air this time and her reaction happen in a matter of seconds. From the passenger's window she reached out the open car window and pulled Nicole by her hair. With her grip on Nicole's hair she calmly stepped out of the car. She switched her grip to untangle Nicole's hair with car door. She dragged Nicole by her hair. Nicole was wildly swinging her fist in the air. Two out of the hundred blows thrown by Nicole land on Mimi's body. Mimi kneed Nicole in the face until blood started pouring from her face. We all screamed. Begging Mimi to stop but she kneed her harder and faster. Bleed splattered on Mimi's jeans as Nicole's begs for mercy sprayed into the air. Nicole's pleads enforced my prays to the heavens to conclude the darkness of Mimi. Nicole hands stop fighting back and laid lifeless at the sides of her body. With Nicole body at a standstill, Mimi didn't cut the blows short. The shockwave of the hits transcended through each of us. My eyes had to be playing tricks on me. We were looking with our mouths open in disbelief.

"OH MY GOD! YOU FUCKING KILLED HER! YOU FUCKING KILLED HER!" Erica repeated herself like she was convincing her brain to believe what her eyes had just witnessed. Erica's trembling hand pulled out her cell phone to call for help. Her vision blared with tears made it hard to unlock the phone. Erica held her phone up to sky in search of a signal to make the call. Out of nowhere Mimi struck Erica in the back of the head with rock the size of a dictionary. The sound of cracking egg amplified echoed off the trees. I didn't even see it coming Erica didn't even have a chance. Erica drop straight down on her face while touching the leaking open gash in the back of her head. I took a step toward Erica's motionless body but Mimi gave me a stare that could kill. Mimi lift up Erica's dead weighted legs and dragged Erica's limp body by her ankles over to Nicole's stiff body. Nicole's face is a bloody mangled mess. The bloodstained mush which was once Nicole's face made my stomach cringed and everything inside of it flew to my mouth. Dom held the bag under my face to catch my stomach's upset with his right hand and pushed my fly away hairs back out of the way with his left hand. Dom not only looking out for Mimi, he also took care of us all in different ways.

"So, ya'll just going to stand there? Some fucking help please!"

Mimi's yelling hurts my hearing. Free jumped to get the gallon of gasoline out the truck of the car and Tricia rushed to get the long stick strike matches from the glove compartment. As much as my mind told my legs to move they just wouldn't obey. I couldn't take my eyes off of Erica and Nicole's bodies just laying on top of each other. The color had escape their skin and they appeared to be dull. Mimi rid Erica and Nicole bodies of the rings on the fingers, the chain off their necks and the watches off their waist. Dom searched for money in their jean pockets and in their purses. As I watched Mimi and Dom movements, it was a well performed routine. They have practice on more than one occasion, to the point they danced around the bloody bodies like it was second nature.

"Ya'll want anything?" Mimi questioned us as she took the red bottoms off Nicole's dead feet. Tricia helped herself to Nicole's red leather jacket, surprisingly there wasn't any blood on it.

"Y'all good?

Mimi than picked up the rock with the blood spot on it and lift it over her head and hammered it down on Erica's head. I flinched as if the rock was coming down on my head. Through squinted eyes I viewed bloody chucks of skull and brain fragments sprayed into the air, splashing on Mimi's face, chest and hands. She repeat the head banging with the rock to Nicole's head. Free poured the gasoline on the dead bodies as Mimi ordered her to. Tricia systematically lit a match and tossed the lit match on unconsciousness figures. A fire jumped off the bodies into the air about four feet high. Mimi stripped out of her bloody tee shirt, her bleeding jeans and her blood splattered #6 black and white Jordans. She tossed her clothes and sneakers into the fire. Dom pours a gallon of water over Mimi's naked body to rinse the red off her skin but we all could see her dirt. We all had played our part and was ready to go but

Mimi didn't want the fire to spread. We had to wait until the fire dies down before leaving it unattended. Free, Tricia and myself was all baffled. Mimi had compassion for the trees and grass and was willing to protect them from the fire but didn't have a care for the humans in the fire. As the fire blazed up to the sky Dom passed around a bottle of liquor and face masks. Myself, Free and Tricia sat on the out skirts of the fire. We had vacant wet eyes but our heart was overflowing with heavy emotions. Tricia lay in front of the fire like the diva she is. She is laying on her side with her right hand planted on the grass supporting her body up right. Tricia eyes spray grief down her face. Her vision showed how she met Erica and Nicole. It was her first day of cashier training at Bloomingdales from 5pm to 9pm. She was already drained from getting into it with Mimi over Lippa. Mimi didn't think it was a good idea for Tricia and Lippa to get involved. In spite of the fact they clearly liked each other. Mimi forbid it and that was the end of it. But Tricia feelings for Lippa didn't stop. Tricia carried that bag to the training. She thought she was going to at least have a good time at the training but the females at the training shaded her cause she shined too bright. Her fashion sense was born into her bones and face art skills was self-taught. Tricia walked into training with heels, tight black skirt, silky white blouse, hair laid and face beat to the gods. For a sixteen year old she put plenty woman to shame. The room was cold as the instructor stared. In train class Tricia sat alone and when it was break time she ate alone out the shade. Tricia wish she could bring Mimi to work for just one day so she could handle the snickers as she walk pass or to confront the rumors that spread about her. When Erica and Nicole sat next to her during break on the three week, they were a bright lights in a dark tunnel. They embraced Tricia. Teaching her all types of tricks to aid her fashion addiction by finger feeding it with the BOGO rule, buy one get one. They also schooled her on how to be paid for hours never worked. Erica and Nicole were fun and exciting to Tricia she just want to share the feeling with her friends. But Mimi created tension from introduction cause she was force feeding Lippa to Nicole. Mimi could read the irritation in Tricia eyes but it didn't stop Mimi. The blazing flames burn in Tricia's eyes wishing she could take back the day she brought Erica and Nicole into Mimi's wrath. On the right side of Tricia is Free. Free is squatting in front of the flames. Her head is bowed like she was praying. Inside the fire is Free's heart. Free don't have a filter she thinks out loud...

"Before you came into my life I was twisted about my sexual preference, fearing judgmental eyes, or the talks. People trying to convince me that what I feel ain't real. Dealing with overbearing attitudes just for being me. You made the confusion disappear. Every time I made your beautiful face smile my heart sings. My happiest moments were with you by side. With you by my side I'm invisible. I can overcome any darkness with your brightness. No matter what I was going through you just kept loving me. Loving me for who and what I am. It felt so good sometimes it hurts. I love feeling, breathing and living you. We have come a long way from where we began. I will forever love you. Our memories I will cherish. You will always be a part of me cause a piece of my heart will always belong to you..."

As the words fell from Free's heart she realized the one thing she was worried about the most really wasn't such a big deal cause everybody close to her already knew. Being dangerously in love with Erica wasn't a secret. The person that held her hand was no long around and there was no way of reaching out to her. Free questioned herself how would she make it through this thing called life without Erica by her side. Free wish she would of stood up to Mimi and save her heart from breaking. The expression on their face told what the flames ignited in their minds, the fight for understanding and forgiveness. I sat on the left side of Free. I had my legs crossed Indian style. The hot glow over the bodies showed me a time in my life when every detail made sense. Back when I was a child, before Mimi removed all my innocence from me and my parents share special moments. I saw the Sunday afternoon picnics, the Saturday morning cartoon and the laughter. My father would lift me up in the air and spin me around, it was like having a personal ride on demand. Anytime I was sad my mother would do something outrageously funny to make me laugh just to comfort me. The fire then just like the fire now changed everything, including me. My mother was gone, forever. Every night before I fall asleep late at night I would listen to my father's room door. I can hear him weeping for my mother. It broke my heart to hear a strong man becoming so weak. I'd pray for my mother's return for my father more than I prayed for myself. We both needed her but my father needed her more. He just wasn't the same man without her. I wish god would send my father the only woman he ever loved and maybe he could love me again. Each night I dreamed of the fatherly love I was missing. The smell of hot tar sulfur, burning hair, mixed with the burnt meat unseasoned topped with charred rubber rise in the air out of the fire. The distinctive scent of burning flesh is a smell that will stick with me. Acrid smoke is blocking my airways down to my lungs. The smolder started irritating our eyes and noses, the nonstop crying didn't help. It took two hours and forty seven minutes for the bodies to be a completely pile of flaming ash. Dom handed out face mask to protect us from the toxins in the air but the burnt flesh scent crept pass the mark. The burnt flesh aroma floated in the air blistering our heart. Mimi and Dom were lip locking, caressing each other's skin, like the flames in front of them were romantic in some way. The sight of them displaying affection sickened us all. We all were ready to go.

"Ya'll still want to going to Calvin party? I bet I get $500 easy for these red bottom. What y'all think? Mimi's words shows she has moved forward like nothing happened.

Seven years later...

ONE

Chuck slammed the front door to our condo apartment behind him after he had entered. I felt the breeze on the back of my legs. I didn't turn round to face the steam he was puffing out his nose. I knew he had an attitude I could hear it in his movement. The tricky part was figuring out did his attitude brew at work or was it steep at home. I continued to prepare dinner with my back towards the front door. I heard him smash his keys on top of the kitchen's island marble top. The crash between the keys and the marble top startled me. "How was your day?" I tossed the words over my shoulder at him. I only asked out of courtesy. I really didn't want to hear a story in police code. A language I am not fluent in, it all sounds like blah blah blah. Before I could turn around to face his answer. He had walked around the kitchen island and was standing behind me. His breath sweep cross the nape of my neck it felt like a silk scarf grazing my skin. I close my eyes my mind brushed in bliss. He lean forward bringing his tender lips closer to my neck. He gently press his soft lips on my neck and my head couldn't hold up. My head drop down on his left shoulder inviting his lips to taste my flesh. His throbbing manhood press up against my bottom cheeks making it wet between my legs. A creamy moan of affectionate escaped my lips. He tickles me with his warm whispers of words into my ear. His aroused appetite trigger him to suck and bite on my earlobe as his breathe and tongue penetrate my ear canal. I could smell the tension building on his breath. His passion took complete control over his movements. In a blink of my eyes his hand grips both of my hips as his teeth take a supple bite of my shoulder. He then plant an apologetic kiss on the bite spot. I melt under his gentleman manners. His right hand swiftly crossed over my bra covered breast then suddenly and gently slide down under my skirt, pass my underwear. I gasp for air like I jumped into a pool of cold water. His velvety touch roughly massaging my clit in a circular motion setting off a wave dampening his smooth fingertips.

"Oh, my day was filled with surprises. Today I went to Gemini's Flowers at lunchtime to take my beautiful wife my out to lunch to celebrate our 5 year anniversary, SURPRISE! You wasn't there. You know I'm a hopeless romantic so I didn't stop there. I showed up at Joie's school cause there's no doubt MY wife would be there at dismissal, MY wife is faithful, everyday 2:45pm MY wife is front line to pick her Joie up, SURPRISE! NO WIFE again. My wife had set up Joie to go to dance class with her classmate, Lynda, and Lynda's mother. I looked like a fucking idiot standing in the parking lot. So now that you know how my day went please tell me how did your day go or should I say where did you go?

I turn around to offer my apologies to his eyes. I completely forgot today was our anniversary. I took a "me" day. I watch him lick my juices off his index and middle fingers on his right hand. He move in closer my eyes facing his nose. I inhale his lip and sucked on his soft spot with puppy dog eyes. He pin me up against the kitchen cabinets. He twist his left arm around my back. His left hand grip my neck from behind something like being in a clutch. His hold consents limited breathing capability. He drags his face down the right side of my face. His breathe slides down my skin sending vibrations down my spine. The combination of his cold nose and heated breath on my skin turns me on. As his tongue dance in my mouth he release his clamp on my spine. His strong hands lift me up onto the counter by his hold on my hips. His hands and his mouth taste my flesh from chest to stomach. He pop open every button on my egg shell white shirt. My moans begs for the touch of his lips or manhood. He bites my lips for begging, it's not lady like. He rams his right hand's index and middle fingers between my vagina's walls while speaking through his gritted teeth as intense punishment.

"A "me" day" I feel like I'm living with a fucking stranger in my house.

Your house? I thought this was a home we built together. He removes his finger and grab a handful of my hair with his left hand. He pulls me down off the counter top by my hair. A weeper fell from my lips for the sting that came alone with his tug on my hair. He use the back his right arm to wipe the top of the kitchen island clear. The clashing of wooden bowls with the floor made a big settling sound. The hand cut green and red peppers scattered across the floor. He used his hold on me to turn me away from facing him. He then bent me over the cleared island's marble countertop, smash the front of my body down. The coolness of the marble countertop under my chest and my stomach is soothing. His pants rubs my skin down. The air blowing from his lips shadows down my spine and pricks my insides. He kicks my legs open and made my privates public. Silent cries were in the air from the brutality. With his left hand tugging my hair and his right hand planted where my back and ass met, he force his stiff night stick into my wet tunnel. In the midst of the sexual raid I reach both of my hands forward grabbing hold of oxygen I needed cause I was short winded.

"Yes, My house, I'm trying to figure you out. You've changed so drastically. I don't even recognize you. You gotta be someone else.
You use to adore me, you would never

ignore me. Forgetting our anniversary? This is the second time this week Joie has went with Lynda to dance class. Tell me what's going on with you?"

What's going on with me? You ain't leaving no kisses behind when you walk out the door every morning. Goodbye with no words. If these walls could talk they would have nothing to tell. No words just shadows walking around. There's no way you could be who you say you are. You've checking my clothes, my whereabouts, I wonder if you've ran my fingerprints already. You question every move I make but you the one with scratches on your back. I'm convinced there's an intruder in MY house. My words fueled his manhood aggression. His night stick strokes turned to ruthless stabs to my insides. His vicious grip on my hair pulled my head back lifting my torso up off the marble countertop. I was facing him upside down, my mouth open grasping for air. His strong hot words danced over my face.

"The suspense is pounding and clouding up my head, please tell me you'll never lie to me!"

The love was gripping off his words. Before I could answer him, he shove his tongue down my throat. He delivers hardhearted stabs to my insides with a coldblooded stare from his eyes making me warm on the inside and cold on the outside. My eyes close it's too chilly. He tug harder on my hair curving my backbone backwards. He immediately ask for forgiveness by showering my skin with sweet wet kiss. I beg for more punishment by backing up and raining on his stick. His back shot kisses spinal all the way through my whole body pass my skin. We climax together. He release his hold on my hair and I fell on top of the cool marble countertop. He collapse his dead weight on my back from the explosion. His phone starts ringing right after we finished. He reach down to his ankles to retrieve his phone from his pants pocket. He answers. I begin to put my clothes back in place, pulling my skirt out of a roll around my waist and re-buttoning my blouse. He held his hand over the phone, his version of mute. He pulls two pieces of paper out of the inside pocket of his blazer. He place the folded paper on the kitchen countertop and hammer his fist on top of paper. He looked me dead in my eyes and I could see the fiery behind his death stare.

"We'll discuss this tonight!"

And he left. I watch his back walk out the front door. This was the usual actions after a fuck fight. His schedule don't allow time for both, so we fuck and fight at the same time, not conventional but practical. I opened up the first piece of paper. It is Joie original Birth Certificate. I knew the truth but the lie was staring at me in black and white. The second folded paper is a family court subpoena for parental visitation rights, partitioned by Domonique Thomas. OMG! Domonique Thomas is name I haven't heard in seven years. Domonique Thomas is a part of my past. A past I have buried deep. The memorial to my high school days happened when I was eighteen years old. Chuck would never understand, that my past is not picture perfect like the wedding photos on the side of our bed. I have to find Mimi...

My mind starts surfing as my body wave through the penthouse condo. I fell in love with the condo four years ago solely of the skyline view. Straight ahead from the front door is the living room with a window wall. Windows that start at the ceiling and end at the floor. The outlook make me consider the possibility of walking off the edge of the hard wood living room floor right across the Hudson River into the hills of trees on the opposite side. This view has the power of capturing my attention for hours. Eyeballing the sunrays dancing on the water is relaxing as well as hypnotizing. The view transport my mind hours away from New York when I never left. The first floor sparkling wood floors was just the icing on the cake. The black and white marble planks took the cake. Chuck was worried about Joie and the plank staircase cause there are no rails. But I was already in love willing to live around any obstacle. After condo searching for six months this was the best by far. The plank staircase is to the left of the front door. Under the high end of the planks is a door to rectangle shaped laundry room. Around the corner from laundry room is the living room's back wall facing the beautiful window wall. To the far left is the downstairs bathroom. But before you get to the bathroom there's a door under lock and key. Behind the door is a room I haven't seen or been in since we moved in here four and half years ago, its Chuck's office. Across from the stunning planks stairs is the kitchen. A cooking facility equipped with all modern technology thanks to the wedding gift. Besides money we were given strictly kitchen appliances. Chuck's evil spirited mother put the word out that I don't cook. So family and friends felt the need to help out. I'm not her number one draft pick for her son. The theme in the kitchen is weaved baskets. When I was a kid I love the fall cause every fall we went apple picking and pumpkin picking as a family with our weave baskets hooped on our arms. The marble top island separated the kitchen from the living room's open space. I put four leather weaved bar chairs on the outside of the island with the matching circle shaped leather weaved chandelier. Glass stove tops and dishwasher both with timers illuminated the kitchen, it was a different living than the tenement studio apartment I hailed from. The living room is the heart of the condo. The window wall mirrors the mind and spirit. If the sunny rays fills the room it warms my insides. When the moonlight bounce off the walls it set my thoughts to rest. Nature is so powerful I had to add décor to accentuate the beauty that flowed through the living room. Between Chuck's office door and the downstairs bathroom door is a sparkling wooden console, on top of the console is a children's poem book. As a child my mother would read to me from it every night. I found it badly burnt floating alone side the curb after the house fire was extinguished. It was open to the last poem she read to me "This is a house were children live" written by Judith Bond. I laugh now cause the most memorable parts of the poem were my mother's adlibs. I saved the book and had it dipped in gold so I could always keep the memory fresh like flowers. If I get to close to the book I could smell the smoke from that fatal memory. Above the console I hung an extra-large wood canvas designed with abstract art. The inlay of seashells and pieces of mirror glass were set on the wood by a genius to resemble peacock feathers. I could stare at the beauty of the canvas for hours but the hidden treasure was how the sunlight danced off the pieces of mirrors. The tango reflection on the wall creates an indoor oasis. The abstract art inspired me. I transformed one of my own flower drawings by adding broken pieces of a mirror to draw attention to the elegance of a blooming flower. I hung my art on the left wall of the living room over the fifteen minutes to midnight blue colored sofa. The velvety upholstery felt like sitting on a cloud. It was so nice I had to buy it twice. I put the second sofa on the left side of the first one. The second sofa was face the window wall. Creating a nice little walkway between the leather bar chairs and the second sofa. I also produced an idol triangle shape space between the arms of the two sofas. I put a glass end table with a white and silver mosaic base lamp on top. Not only was the sofa soft and comfortable the nail head trim on the sofa also played in the sunlight making the common lounge experience heavenly. Across the room on the opposite wall is the entertainment center. Sitting in the middle of the room is a large round glass coffee table. I dressed the coffee table with a white and sliver decorative mosaic letter tray and tall vase. I always have fresh flowers. Owning a flower shop helps. The scent of fresh flower is the scent of new beginnings. Over the coffee table is an oversize chandelier mimicking the shape of sun, brighten the space. A stainless steel ball with many rods of steel in all different sizes stemming from the ball. There is light at the end each one of the uneven rods. If the sun wasn't shinning outside I could turn on similar sunlight inside. The whole left wall was blocked by a hundred inch television sitting on a sparkling wooden book case. I really didn't want to put any furniture in front of the wall window but immediately fell in love when I spotted the matching chairs to the sofa but they only had raincloud grey. The high arm rest made the chairs favor the inside of my mother's plush jewelry box. I bought two of them and place them in front of the wall window with a compass side table in the middle. I position the jewelry box chairs sideways. I get lost in my head while my eyes inhale the view. The compass is nice décor but it there to give me direction while surfing the waves in the sky. Straightening up the condo seemed like a good idea to take my mind of the two pieces of paper Chuck presented me with. With a laundry basket of clean clothes in my hand I walked up the marble planks to the second floor of the condo. The second floor was covered in fox fur. As the fur tickle through my toes imitating the softness I imagine cloud to be. The window wall extended to the second floor. But the window wall was slit in between the two bed rooms. In my room the window wall extended to left wall of the room. From the left side window wall I could see the George Washington Bridge. At night when the bridge light up it appears the stars have gather around the bridge's ends to hold it up in the sky. The condo is just up the river from the El Barrio creek I'm from but seem light years apart. I place my queen size bed in the middle of the window walls. Chuck couldn't understand why I didn't want rails on the bed. The bed is my cloud floating in the glass sky, thanks to window walls on both sides of the bed. Rails on the bed takes away from the levitating experience, even cheapening the flight. The formed triangle at the head of the bed was filled with a huge turquoise and sliver vase containing silk cherry blossom tree branches. The vase is for the sunlight to waltz with. The silk cherry blossom are for me. The sight of flowers over my head when my eyes open is spiritually moving. To the right of the bed was a turquoise with charcoal undertones wooden dresser. Naturally the right side is Chuck's side, leaving the left side to me. On the back wall of my bedroom is a smaller version of turquoise with charcoal undertones wooden dresser and on top is a sixty inch television. On the right side of the television is the door to the bedroom bathroom. The bathroom walls were all mirrors. I went in the bathroom put fresh towels on the racks. I stare at my reflection. Gawking back at me is solid black business high heel pumps, nude colored stockings, a pale tangerine colored knee high pleaded skirt on the bottom and an egg shell white button up blouse with an lengthy collar that ties into a bow on top. With this type outfit I braided my hair at night and leave them til morning and then loose them out. I do this just to have a wiggly hair day since my outfit is so straight. On workdays I usually have on a pair flats, black leggings with a floral printed pin tucked front yoke tunic and my signature bun of hair on the back of my head. I frown at the image. It didn't have style and glare like Mimi but dullness is my style. I went next door just to peek into Joie's room. Joie's bright yellow room, her favorite color. I pick Joie's slept in pajamas up off the area rug in front of her bed. She's seven years old with a fifth grade reading level but picking up after herself is a concept she's has yet comprehend. I let her decorate her room to her liking. She picked the crown headboard twin size day bed. I couldn't have made a better choice. When the sunlight comes in from the window wall it dance of the head broad decorating the room like a disco inferno. Most of her toys are plastic kitchen appliances, she loves cooking. I smile to myself every time I see her toaster alarm. It pops fake toast out when it sounds, it's just too cute. I fell in love with her TV that's almost identical to an oversized microwave. I won a ton of hugs and kissed when I stumbled into the TV, a perfect fit. Just the thought of Joie's smile brightens my day. I found myself back downstairs after tidying up Joie's bathroom. I start to clean up the chopped peppers of the wooden floor, the residue of me and Chuck's episode. I sat a pot of water on the glass top stove for the pasta. My nerves were on edge cutting up pepper might leave with no fingers. Running a business, looking after a child, and preforming the loving wifely duties is a job where there's no punch out clock. Now to add Dom to plate is more than I can eat. I have to get to Mimi... I remember the first time Mimi actually talked to me. It was the first day of high school. She walked by me laughing "You a long way from the playground, girly." were the words she said through her laughter. After she spoke she throw her lit cigarette butt to the floor. She stomped it out with her right foot, winked and smiled at me. At that very moment I noticed me. I started comparing my Hannah Montana t-shirt to Mimi's crop top t-shirt. And since I was eyeing her shirt I noticed I didn't have breast like she had. I didn't have to do much comparing thanks to my peers. They were kind enough to point out every flaw I had from head to toe, on the daily. It was funny how they had the time to discuss my short comings but wouldn't hold a conversation with me. Normal kids would turn to their homes for guidance and acceptance but I lived with my father, my mother had passed away. My father is still heartbroken from the loss of my mother. It felt like he refuse to love again even me, his own kid. Don't get me wrong I never wanted for anything. Every

Saturday I had a standard hair, nails and feet appointments since I could remember. My mother was my chaperone but since she been gone I made my own way to Ms. Carla's, all by myself. My father was conditioned to put food money in the green envelope and laundry slash dry cleaning money in the red envelope, just like he did when Mama was here. Both envelope were pinned to the fridge by magnets. I did the food shopping, the cooking, laundry and every Saturday morning I drop my father's uniforms off at Mr. Chung's cleaners. I practically take care of myself and my Dad. My father is a mailman. He leaves every morning at 5:30 am. When my alarm would pull me from my dreams at 7 am there's always a "Good Morning" note and five dollar bill waiting for me on the kitchen counter. Me and my father get out of school and work at the same time but he usually gets home at 7 pm every night. He goes to JoJo's bar to swim in a bottomless cup of his lost. After the first three months of high school I was falling into a hole of hopeless. I was really missing my mother, the lost was still fresh and it was the one time in my life I really need her. I would've killed for a just one hug from her loving arms. I was really depressed. Humans need human interaction just like they need air. I spoke 10 times a day, I said "Good Morning" to the bus driver, I would say "Here" each time in all 8 of my classes. Then I said "Good Afternoon" to the bus driver on my ride home. I wondered if I was a good cook cause my Dad never eats. The night before my life changed forever I fell asleep watching Disney's® Chicken Little. My clock radio went off at 7 am, blasting Gloria Gaynor's voice singing "I Will Survive." I started dancing like I was in kindergarten. Singing and dancing in the morning before school was me and my mother morning routine. For 5 minutes my mother was in the room with me. I could feel her. I could smell her. It wasn't the first time I felt my mother's presences but it was the one time I truly needed it. I could hear her voice all the way from heaven saying, "Don't like it? Then change it!" those words are my mother's motto. I got ready for school in the best pieces of clothes I owned and topped it with my mother's sweater. I wasn't ready to leave her spirit behind. And I just couldn't spend one more day alone. This sweater was the only thing I had saved from the fire. Her scent was weaved into the fabric. I had $1,375 dollars and 64 cent saved up. I had decided that day I was going to change my life. I was fixed on asking Mimi to take me clothes shopping after school. I no longer wanted to be as the elementary refugee in high school. Giving up being well-known for sporting Hannah Montana's t-shirts, underwear and backpack. Being acknowledged for the rainbow colored Sketcher® on my feet and the Children's Place glitter pants covering my legs was a thing of the past starting that day. I will be just like the normal teenager or at least dressed like one. I could already feel the change happening as I walked to the bus stop that morning. I flew off the bus when I spotted Mimi from the bus. I was storming up to her with my mother's sweater of confidence. Fear of rejection calmed my walking pace over to Mimi, I eased into a lady like poise. With my face and hand sweating I didn't want to look thirsty. "Let me get this right, you want me to dress you?" I nodded like a bobble head. I couldn't believe she agreed so easily. The only problem was she wanted to go right then. I was concerned about missing a day of school. I hadn't missed a day since pre-k. It was a recorded that I was very proud of and didn't want to mess up my chances of winning the district award, again this year. "The choice is yours, you can be attendance award winner or social loser?" I've been the district attendance winner it comes with a ceremonial dinner and a trophy. But the best part was having my mother at my side. My father tried filling in as a date but drinking at Jojo's was more important to him. For the last two previous years he missed it and I went with Ms. Janet, our neighbor. And I've been the social loser for the past three months and I didn't like it at all. So I decided to ditch school for the first time in my life. Mimi knew I needed to go shopping and I really wanted to but missing school was eating me alive. I asked Mimi what happens when she ditched school, I didn't want to offend her but this was normal behavior for her, clearly. Her movements told she was unbothered by missing school. I voiced my concerns about not being familiar with the school procedures. Do the school contact parents? She shushed me with a GYN doctor's note pad out her backpack. "When you give this note to the counselor tomorrow morning your absent will be excused and they won't contact your parents, cause the type of doctor. So relax and I'm about to change your life." I smiled at her, at that moment I didn't know how true her words really were. I didn't want to get in any trouble. "1st off, why don't you wear a bra? You do know people can see your nipples?" I didn't wear a bra cause I didn't know I needed to wear one. "Damn, we have to start from scratch." We went to Victoria's Secrets® on 34th street. I bought 4 bras and 10 panties for $160. Mimi demanded that I walk out the store with a bra and a pair of panties on. She literally burn my Hannah Montana underwear on a side street. We then ran up and down 34th street. Dipping in and out of various stores. We tried on different types of cloths, hats and custom jewelry. I bought some things and chuckling at others things. I laughed until my cheeks hurt and my side was aching. I haven't had that much fun in a long time. It felt good to just be lighthearted. We shopped for 8 hours and I spent $800 dollars, an average of a hundred dollars every hour but the feeling that came with the experience was priceless. When I looked in the mirror in the dressing room to see the new me. I looked just like Mimi. I had white Jordan's on feet. Mimi had the same sneakers on her feet in black. I had on tight True Religion jeans in red and Mimi had on the same ones on in black. I had a white crop top and Mimi had on the same shirt in red. We took a picture on the street and the photographer asked were we twins, cause of our favorable facial features. I laughed at the man but when I saw the picture it looked like a picture with special effects. Like it was a one person double to stand back to back. The photographer asked again and Mimi answered yes. From that very moment my name changed from Gemini, GeGe, for short to Mimi's Twin. Even taking the 6 train uptown to 125th street was an advantage. Mimi spotted people's funny movements, for my entertainment. I think it was her way of showing me it was okay to be different. It was pass dismissal time at school, I had my fun and was ready to return to the comforts of my world. Mimi denied my request. We were going to meet up with her boyfriend, street name Dom born Domonique Thomas. Dom is big and scary with a raspy voice equivalent to a cigarette chain smoker. Clearly he is older than Mimi. Dom wasn't too bright so if any one talked over his comprehension he start communicating with his oversized fist. From that day to the night in Brentwood we were each other's shadows. Mimi made my awkward high school years the best spontaneous four years of my life. There were moments I was so scared I almost piss my pants. Periods when I've seen the most disgusting things. Sickening minutes that made me throw up but the retention forever embedded in me. I've witness thing that a person couldn't imagine in their wildest dreams or most frightening nightmares. With Mimi every day is an adventure or a disaster. Mimi is everything I'm not. She's loud and animated and I'm a quite wall flower. I love to watch her in action. It was like watching a ballet. Her movement her mannerisms all telling an in sync story. My thoughts of the past was broken by the ring of the doorbell. It was Lynn, Lynda's mother, with Lynda in one hand and Joie in the other. Joie greeted me with a hug. She squeeze me so tight around my neck with her little arms. It was amazing how such a little body could contain so much love. I thanked Lynn for the favor and promised to return the gesture at her request. I sent Lynn downstairs to her apartment six floors down. I started dinner over and begun Joie's homework. Joie is so smart. I just watched as she figure the instructions out. She read the directions, sounding out the unfamiliar words. The words slipping past her adorable gap tooth smile. I feel in love with her little face on sight. Her little button nose and her sprinkling eyes stole my heart. We had dinner together with a deep conversation about her day at school. Apparently Ms. White, her teacher, is a drama queen. Ms. White melted down over spilled milk accord to Joie. Joie possessed the same gift as Mimi to retain a person's attention for hours. Joie talked until her eyes closed. I kiss her forehead and pulled the cover up to her chin. I planned to be in bed by the time Chuck crawled back in the condo and stay asleep until he crept out in the morning. Explaining that I had never had sex with Domonique Thomas was going to be hard to argue with his name embedded on the Birth Certificate. Then trying to explain that I'm not Joie's biological mother, even though I'm the only mother she knows, will really take him for a loop. After our wedding Chuck wanted to adopt Joie to be her legal father. I killed the idea by telling him it wasn't my decision to make. I jumped from the flashback of Chuck slapped down Joie's birth certificate as evidences of my lie. It's hard to argue what's in black and white. I need to rest tomorrow I have to track Mimi down. The last time I set eyes on Mimi she handed Joie's newborn body over to me before disappearing. I wonder what the others are up to...

***

Upstairs above Gege's flower shop is a studio apartment. When Gege hired Amy, as her assistant Gege throw in the apartment as a bonus. Amy was a perfect fit for Gege's business. Amy was born with a green thumb. Besides growing astonishing flowers she grow vegetables in the mini greenhouse in the store's backyard. I use my key to enter Amy's studio apartment. On the right side of the front door is the bathroom. Further to the right in small rectangle kitchen. A few steps forward is the living room area. She had a big Pac-man yellow sofa with the back facing the door. She won extra points with me by having a cherry, pretzel, apple and pear shaped throw pillows lining the sofa. Across from the Pac-man sofa is enormous oval bookshelf creating a sectional between the living room and the bedroom. In the middle of book shelf sat a 60 inch TV. The coolest part of the TV is it swings around according to which room needs entertainment. Above and below the TV are shelves stacked with books, the real amusement. The various book titles dressing the shelf were the most intriguing. She had books about the civil right fight, home remedies, vegan cookbooks and romantic novels. The shelf is a cupboard of food for the mind. I could feast all day. My mind has a bottomless hunger for knowledge. On the right wall of the living room in front of the windows, between the yellow sofa and the oval book shelf are four single Pac-man ghost chairs stuck on blue after Pac-man gulped down a power pellet. In the center of it all was a super cool coffee table with a face from pac-man's game. With all the aspects of a broad in the game, pebbles lining the twist and turns. She has plenty of retro cool furniture. For example, the orange and strawberry shaped fur bean bags placed in front of the living room's left wall. Behind the bookshelf is the homemade bedroom. Stepping into the bedroom it's a complete turnaround from the living room, it the enchanting indoor forest. Covering the bedroom floor space, from wall to wall, is a grass like carpet. Walking across the carpet barefooted is parallel grazing in an open country field. The nature scent of wildlife is coming from the spider plants she had on the window seals on both side of her bed. The vines has crawled up the window frame and was making it's to the wall behind the bed. The thick padding snow white headboard with individual diamonds embedded in it sat between the two windows facing the oval bookshelf. Laying on the snow white cotton soft bed is akin to resting on a cloud. On the right wall is a wooden closet with doors stolen from some medieval castle. On the right wall is three large pieces of unshaped wood positioned to resemble a table. Sitting on the corners of the fake wooden table are two huge devil's ivy plant. The ivy's vines have scaled up the wall, across the ceiling and drop amid air over the bed. Amy lived in the light of sun by day and at night she dance in candle light. When her room is illuminated by the candles the plant wildlife breathe fresh air into my soul. The apartment is corky and cutie just like Amy. "Free..." she yells my name as she runs to jump in my arms and start planting kisses on my face. Amy is naturally over attentive. She unties my black construction boot, gently remove my foot from the boots. She massage my socked feet one at a time. While questioning me about my day, her eyes waits for the answers. I truly didn't want to get deep into politics of my day but it just slips out sometime. Today was a scheduled protest for the Free Warriors. I ask was Martin Luther King's coldblooded murder in vein? Every time I turn on the TV I'm forced to hear the rhetoric fly out this permanent face painted clown with the most fucked up weave I've ever seen and I've seen some messy kitchen hair dos but his by far is the worst. It's unconstitutional to single out a religion or sex. But yet America allow this bigot to announce travel bands to Muslims and banding transgenders from the army. While screaming "Making America great again." which America does he speak of? Cause the last time I check white America has always been in good standing. You know scalping Indians robbing them of their land and then enslaving black folks to build on the stolen property. When was it bad for them? Cause I definitely missed it. He out here on twitter thugging, starting wars with foreign countries and clouding up the news feed with alterative facts. He boast about the fact he signed fifty pieces of legislation but leave out he rolled back fifteen of Obama's administration rules and regulation. And the fucking idiot did it out of pure spite, no merit to his actions. I tell you how I know... are you ready? Cause its common sense! Obama's aimed to keep the mentally ill from the ability to purchase gun. The asshole rolled that back. Please tell me who wants a mentally challenge person to own a gun, legally? Or how about drug testing for unemployment benefits? Whether on drugs or not you worked for those benefit, if you didn't know it's deducted from your pay check. He is way out of his league but they keep cheering him on. Amy suggests a bath to calm my nerves. Trump sets me off every time. Excuse me I'm just use to them wearing their hoods at night not during the day. Of course she undress me while the tub filled with water. She leads the way to the tub of warm water with assorted colored flower petals floating on top, waiting on me. I love bathing at her apartment the old school free standing tub with the four feet, is just my style. Plus the tub is big enough for two. I encouraged her to join me. Her skin is soft and genuine just like her personality. Some might say her brain cells are fried from all the marijuana she smoked. But they would be wrong her brain cooked up many brilliant ideas. She's book smart and the brains are amazing. Besides her beautiful smile that can light up a room, we had a lot of things in common. We both were vegans, most of the vegetables she grows, she eats and our favorite channel is CNN. While she bath me she feeds me fresh fruit while puffing on seeds from earth, the whole time. Amy has an unlimited supply of weed. I wonder if Gege even noticed the weed bushes growing outdoor in the store's garden. After the bath Amy had matching bath robes laid out for us. She serves dinner, puree asparagus topped with balsamic vinegar sautéed tofu and mixed peppers. Amy had already eaten so while I devour my home cooked dinner she braids my hair into cornrows going toward the back. She sat on the edge of bed and I sat in between her naked legs. As earthy as Amy is her legs are always nicely shaved. In between shoving food into my mouth I rest the right side of my face on her inner tight. Her softness eases my roughness, setting me free. She provides emotional support with her caring touches. There wasn't nothing Amy wouldn't do for me and me for her. She is open and honest, traits that's hard to find in people know a days. We shared something so common but still so rare. I've never been here before. I've dated different women and never came close to anything like this, not even with Erica. Erica is my first love and no matter what, will always have a piece of my heart. That puppy love had me overly infatuated with Erica. I kind of followed her around. But by being with her I became comfortable in my own skin and more comfortable next to another woman's skin. Experiencing Erica is something I'll never forget. Coming in contact with Amy is an interaction that effected my whole body. It's completely something different, she the sweet breeze on a hot summer day, she's the warm feeling in the stomach when you wake up to a "good morning beautiful" text. Yeah, I know Mimi send me to look after Gege and Amy wasn't part of the original plan. But with Amy it's so authentic, it has to be the real deal. She knows who I am and she accepts that. I know I'm in too deep and wasn't allowed to fall in love. But I can't get enough of Amy. I spend at least three nights a week at her studio apartment. If she wanted me too I'll be her girly girl, paint my nails and wear a pair of heels. We both fell out laughing cause there's no way in heaven, earth or hell I'll have heels on my feet.

"Hey bae, I have some tickets to event at Studio Museum in Harlem are you interested?"

Here we go... I hate not being able to give her the one thing she really wanted but being seen publicly is just not foreseeable. Now is just not safe. I wasn't ready to explain the democracy of making such a publication nor did I think she would truly understand all the elements of my existence. I can't be catnapping under Amy, I have to stay woke. Mimi is coming I can feel it. Mimi is like the sister you love dearly but can't stand her guts. Mimi can be a beautiful person but when she gets ugly, she gets dangerous. Mimi is like a hurricane fire ball leaving behind devastation that never heals. She always have something creeping from under her sleeve and I will never be caught snoozing.

"Bae, have you been taking you meds? I only ask cause you seem a little tense tonight."

I try to nod her off but she tugged my head so I could look her in the eyes as I answered her. I complained that she tugged a little too hard on my hair as she braided my hair. She immediately apologized for the unintentional affliction of pain. I didn't have the heart to disappoint her twice in one night. I haven't been taking no meds. They put me in a daze and I need to be on my toes, alert ready for whatever. Being fully prepared for Mimi arrival. Gege is completely clueless about many thing but Mimi unexpected arrival is far from her mind, and Tricia is so self-centered she's oblivious to the entire world, all she see is herself. I think Gege will crumb under a face to face with Mimi. It's my job to be the strong one. The only one that have the ability to reason with Mimi. I can smell the smoke of lies and feel the fire of betrayal being ignited. Amy is no fool. Her eyes were investigating my facial expression. I had to make her feel good enough to close her eyes with pleasure to shield her from the pain. I started with little nibbles on her neck. I love when she tilt her head to side as she blush. My taste bubs surf her skin as she rides the wave pleasure. The riffles rock her to restful place. She fell asleep in my arms as Mel Gibson's give a lesson on the Mayan Kingdom's history titled Apocalypto. Not everybody can handle the subtitles. But I love it. It's the world thru different eyes for me to see. I watch her angelic face in still form and it's more beautiful than her stunning smile in her eyes. She sets me free. Our thing is unconventional but practical. I cuddle with my earth angel til Jaguar was watching me from the television screen.

***

Just kicking it with Dickey is always an amusing, exciting all while having a pleasurable time. I love to just hear him say my name, especially since he nickname me "Trich" today's adventure... He claim to have special surprise for me. So I allowed him to blindfold me inside his work's refrigerated delivery van. I asked a million question at a thousand miles per hour. I try to peek a few times but was caught every time. He pacified me with kisses to my forehead and soft strokes on my hair. When he finally uncovered my eyes, I almost fainted I had died and went to heaven. I was standing in the woman's leather section in the Gucci store. His eyes were smiling cause I was ecstatic. A spring red leather jacket with ruffles around the color down the front, around the bottom and on the edge of the sleeves had stolen my heart. I remember my senior year I wanted a red channel leather jacket I had saved up my money I was a hundred dollars away from actually owning it and Nicole beat me to the purchase. But I ending up with the jacket any way. Too bad Mimi burnt it cause "It's suspicious" I think she was just hating. But now I'm getting a brand new better version. The jacket cost 34 hundred plus 3 more hundred in tax. Dickey wanted to get a belt and shade but it's a New York fact Fab buys out the belts on the reg. But today Dickey was in luck. So add another 4 hundred for his Double G buckle belt. He had to have matching shade with a tag of on another $375. I had to have a shades too. The ones that fit my face where a square frame with red, black and green glitter frame. The grey shaded lens is the last touch of awesomeness. My shades tag was about 6 hundred. Total bill 51 hundred dollars. We both share the vain pettiness of wanting to best dressed. I turned my head when he handed over a credit card to be swiped. My stomach started turning flips and my hand was sweating. I could pretend not to know that Dickey was stealing credit card numbers from his job and wire transferring the money to dummy accounts. And some way he get the money to these cards. But its hard to un-know something. One would think that since I get physically ill every time he use the cards I wouldn't partake see that's where you're wrong the immature level is high and as long as I get what I want the rest don't matter. We walked out of the store with our bag and Dickey was on a super high. He raced me to the van parked two blocks away. I showered his freckled face with kisses. He had given me the best surprise ever, fashion. We took a stroll in central park. We was laughing at the cashier's hating face when we cashed out at the register. We bought hotdogs. His silly self put ketchup on my nose, I try my best to get him back. We tripped on puppy love and he landed on top me. When he wraps his arms around my body it feels as warm as a security blanket. We stared into each other eyes. I wanted him as much as he wanted me but Mimi is coming. And I don't think he's strong enough to handle Mimi. Dickey is at the tender age when everything is a new experiences. Making every single thing a big deal. If he can't find the perfect outfit for school he has a complete male diva break down. His break downs means something else get broke, like a wall, a TV and or a cellphone. Mimi will blow out the lights of innocence in his eyes. Many adults can't take on Mimi, Dickey is a boy, he don't stand a chance. And what happens when the days grow old, cards all fold, image lose it lust and the youthfulness we share has aged. I'm an image dragon forever young at heart. So I dodged the kiss. I suggested he returned to work. I didn't want him to get in trouble for his extended lunch break. He agrees only if I promised to meet him after his shift was over. We shook on the deal. We literally wiggled our bodies as the seal on the agreement. I almost jiggled out of my Beyonce inspired ombre Brazilian wavy virgin lace wig. I can't have my $225 hair hitting the floor and my straight back cornrow be exposed. Yes I wear nice expensive wigs. Besides fashion changing on the daily I have too much personality to commit to a single wig. I stood behind my word and met up with Dickey at midnight. He had a colorful flannel blanket laid out on the roof of the delivery van with pillow propped up on the van's fans. He held his hand out to help aboard the roof. We laid on our backs looking up at the stars. I wish I could live in this moment forever. It's a warm tingling feel from the sky. I was transported to plenty evening share between myself, Mimi, Free, Gege and Dom. We would lay out on the grass under the stars for hour. Drinking to our accomplishment and watching our minor problems go up in smoke. The night air and shinning star calmed the mind through sight. Sharing the moment with Dickey made the moment even more magical. I wish I could freeze time for others.

"By her cleaning my room is an invasion of privacy! I know she's only trying to take care of her son. But I ain't a baby I can clean my own damn room. She's everywhere asking questions just butting in on my every move I make. I leave the house today for legroom and she's blows up my phone. I don't have enough breathing space. She all over me cause I might fail a class and not graduate but the key word is "MIGHT" she had the audacity to confiscate my Gucci sneaker, sneakers she did not pay for mind you, until end of the semester. I wear my personality without my kicks I can't wear my brand new matching Gucci belt and shades. Parents just don't understand. I would've been ok with any other form of punishment just not the Gucci."

I just enjoy watching Dickey mind pace back and forth with his adolescent testosterone drama sprouting from his mouth. His mother is a tad bit noisy. I went to his apartment in Harlem for "Netfix and Chill" we were set to binge the show Bates Motel. I had turn him on to the original 1960's Psyco produced by the infamous Alfred Hitchcock. I totally into psychological horror. Mr. Hitchcock delivers every time. His mother, Ms. Rita, busted in the room over a hundred times. She was out of order over the time laps between us. I know he is often moody thanks to the hormonal and physical changes that usually happens during puberty but like being around him. I nibbled on his cutie anger words and savored the youthfulness taste of his happiness. He was no Lippa. Lippa was a serious hustler. Strictly about his money. I was caught up on the feeling he gave me. A feeling I would never ever forget. A feeling that Mimi took from me. But Dickey is the rainbow after the storm has past. Dickey is so childish. He's known to start a French fry fight in a restaurant or start a juvenile game of name that song, movie or artist at a drop of a dime. Everything is competition. Who can eat the most condiments packages? Who can past the most broads in video games? We flipped a quarter to make 95% of our decisions. What movie to watch? What and where we will eat dinner? Who going to pay for the meal? Being myself, the self-indulgent bitch and irresponsible child is accepted by Dickey. I didn't care about our time difference. So no Dickey is no Lippa, he's much more. He brings the table with a plates of dedication, cups over flow with words of praises and worships all for me to feast on. When I look into his pretty brown eyes I see the innocents shine so bright its blinding. I want to save that light forever and dance in it. I wonder what does he see when he looks into my eyes. Do he see the shallow darkness or can he see where the demons hide? His boyish grin and long-limbed physics leaves me short winded. I try to back away and not let him get too close. Mimi is an evil being and she took Lippa's life to kill my happiness. I just wouldn't be able to live with myself if she take Dickey away from me. Dickey gives me life.

TWO

I woke up feeling tired but I went to bed early last night. I know I had a goodnights rest but I had leftover fatigue. I lose out my braids to have the swiggle look with hopes to impress my high school past. I called Amy, my assistant to drop Joie off at school before tending the shop. Dickey will open up the flower shop and hold down the fort until Amy get there. I had a long day ahead of me and need to start early.

"Why you smiling like a crazy person?" I asked cause her eyes was begging to spill the milk.

"Cause I'm crazy in love."

We both laughed at Amy's illness. I want to be the girlfriend and be nauseated by Amy's hurl of love sickness on my ears but I just didn't have the time. I made a mental note to be prepared to gag on her googly eyes as she spew her love. I wasn't rude but I did push them out the door. Joie walks out the door hand in hand with Amy. I gave her a kiss and hug filled with love. Following my father's tradition Joie will find a "Love U" note in her lunch. I looked in the mirror just to take one last look, before walking out the condo. I took the service elevator to the garage. I hop into my car and drive to the Riverdale Police Department. I had made French toast, sausage, and eggs for breakfast. I decided to take a home cooked breakfast to Chuck as my apology for forgetting our anniversary and sleeping through his presences last night and this morning.

"Oooooh somebodyyy is in trouble!" Nathan, Chuck's partner teased as the squad room noticed my arrival. If I dropped a pin it would be heard. I was trying to offer to stayed and feed him instead of him munching on a plate of files on his desk. Before I could finish my sentence Chuck had a firm grip on my upper right arm. He squeeze my arm so hard I dropped the bag of foggy tupperware filled with his breakfast on the floor next to his desk. He leans in close and talks through his teeth to the top of my head "What the fuck are doing here?" his words felt uncomfortable like the hair dryer's heat got to close to my scalp. As he shuffle me towards a wooden door. He looks both ways before he throws me into the room with a double sided mirror. He toss me so hard my back fell into the metal table bolted to the center of the room's floor. He enters the room and slams the door behind him. I rush him and shower his face with kisses as apologies. I force feed my tongue into his mouth. The intimacy of the kiss caught him off guard. I pull my head away and drag my tongue out his mouth slowly, leaving a salvia string between our lips. I hug him hard with my arm and even harder with my heart. I whisper "Sorry" in his ear and hope his heart hears me. I slide down his body. I smile up at his eyes while lowering down to my knees. Literally preparing to beg for forgiveness. He jerks me up to my feet with authority. He push my back against the wall. He held his right arm over my head with the palm of his hand pin to wall. His jawline is so tight I could see it protruding through his skin. His eyes are dark, strong and particularly piercing through me.

"You can't suck or fuck this away! What the fuck is going on! You fucking Dominque Thomas?" He scream his question into my face. The volume on his voice closed my eyes and cause me to cover my left ear with my left shoulder. The foam that form around his mouth escapes him and lands on my nose and eyelid.

"Waiting for a fucking answer... Is he the reason you won't have my baby?" The palm of his hand lifts off the wall and his fist punch the spot on the wall were his hand was resting. His fist not only cracked the wall but broke me down. I fletch every time he moved a muscle after that. He never put hands on me and I've never seen him so anger before.

"NO!" nor would I ever have sex with Dom! Mimi would burn me for real for that type of betrayal. And to have Chuck's baby I have to get this Mimi thing under wraps. To declare my innocents I had to start with Brentwood and end with Joie. And in between it all is Dom, Mimi, Free and Tricia. But instead of words gushing in the air, tears were streaming down my cheeks. My heart was breaking to see the disappointment in his eyes. I felt the needed to tell Chuck everything but I needed to face my past eye to eye and then I could tell Chuck. I beg for his patience and trust. But from his eyes I know his trust wasn't on the menu. My voice is crackling under the pressure. I had to get out of that room. The wall are closing in on me. I feel trap. In that room I'm no longer his loving wife, I'm an intimidated suspect and was treated as such. I walk out of the room with my head high. I'm going to end my past and get on with my future. I love Chuck and want our marriage to work. I had to get to Mimi... As I walk out of the squad room I could feel eyes groping my body. My little drop by visit just might have bought me some more time. Chuck's mind will be on sex when he gets home. The "Dom" explanation will be on pause. My lawyer, Sharon, told me I had to answer the subpoena. The Riverdale family court building is a few blocks from Chuck's precinct. It's easy to just take care of the damn subpoena now before the past keep spreading. I called Sharon. She was more than willing to see me. I did the floral arrangements for her engagement party some years ago. When

I was served with the subpoena at the shop in front of Amy and customers about three weeks ago I called Sharon. I thought I was keeping it a secret until Chuck slapped me with the subpoena that was served at my condo. Lucky for me Sharon is a family court lawyer and was able and willing to help. Sharon greets me at the second floor elevator as the double doors were opening. I break the ice with a joke about be ready to order her flowers for the wedding. She jokes back if she gets a vacation. She claims to be too busy to use the bathroom much least have time for a ceremony. She's committed to her work getting married is currently on bottom of her "To Do" list. We both laugh it off. She usher me into a conferences room. I took a seat and in minutes another attorney, Tom Bloch, joins us. Before I could say a word he introduces himself as "Joie's" lawyer.

"Why does Joie needs lawyer?" I ask in a very territorial voice cause I need to know why would a seven year old need representation, that's my job.

"She also has a say in the case and the judge don't usually bring small children into the court room." Sharon trying to soothe me by making her voice soft.

"She's 7 years old. She doesn't make decisions for herself, I make the all resolutions in her best interest." I wanted to finish the statement by say I'm the adult in the equation. I've been making all the decisions for the past seven years.

"Ms. Freedom, we all here for the best interest of Joie." Now Tom is offering voice petting.

"I apologize for being defensive, but it's just alarming how this man can come out of JAIL and make demands. He don't know her." I felt the need to fill them in on the facts. They had the look on their face like I should be more open to man wanting to be a part of their child's life.

"That's odd cause she's has been to see him every Christmas for the past 3 years." Sharon's soft voice starts throwing fact daggers. Sharon's words punched me in the throat so hard my chin dropped to my chest and I bit my tongue. Sharon notice the surprise in my eyes. She pause waiting on my response. I had nothing to say, my tongue was hurting too much talk.

"... She was accompanied by your sister Mimi?" As she poke me in my chest with her words of facts she turns the photographs of the prison's visiting log book into eye view.

I had to close my eyes, hold myself together and just think for a second. I had to play along like I was in the know. Every little move I make is being documented and I didn't want to appear like I wasn't looking after Joie. I just sat and nodded the rest of the meeting. What could I say? Mimi is the most sneakiness, outrageously disrespect and just plain evil. When I agree to take care of Joie, we agreed to no interruptions. Children need consistence and I'm to the book. Mimi is rambunctious and dangerous, a child couldn't never be subjected to Mimi. I'm boiling with anger but had to be cool. Mimi is always doing something behind my back.

"Well I'll explain the procedures, by you coming her today, it means you are answering the subpoena, now that you have answered, today you'll get a court date to come back. When you come back we all will be in the court room, me and you, Domonique Thomas and his lawyer and Tom. Tom is going have a private meeting with Joie at her school." Sharon talks freely now that she has shut me up.

"Private? At her school?" I had more to say but this all my swollen tongue would permit.

"Yes, it's necessary to talk to her in a comfortable environment. And the privacy is so her answers are her own. Children tend to try to please their parents. With your presences she'll give the answer she thinks you want her to give. It just procedure. Do you have any questions?"

"Yes what type of questions are going to ask her?"

"Only questions about her position on visiting with her father."

Silence fills the room. Hearing Tom refer to Dom as Joie's father made my teeth clenched. I know he is her father but hearing it made it reality. Sharon broke the air with her question "do you have any questions?" I moved my head from side to side signaling I didn't have any question and I damn sure didn't have anything else to say. The nerve of Mimi? I've never said she can't be a part of Joie's life cause that is far from how I feel but out of common courtesy she should run her movements pass me. After all I'm the one rising her? Do I have a say so in Joie's life? A better question is how did I miss Joie not being around for hours? As mad as I was at Mimi I was disappointed in myself. I instantly stop feeling guilty for putting a microchip in the back of Joie's neck. The microchip hold all Joie's identity information and its service as a GPS. I had it install when she was six months old. One morning I woke up and Joie wasn't in her crib. I lost my mind. I looked high and low with tears blocking my vision. Joie is my reason for living. Looking into her bright eyes feels like I'm getting a second chance at life. Mimi had broken into the apartment through the window in front of the fire escape and took Joie out my tiny apartment to show Joie off at Shug's house. Shug is a sweet heart but her apartment is no place for a child. I vowed to always know where Joie is after that. Cause dealing with the pain of a rubber band around my heart ever minute she wasn't by my side was too great to bare. I know a microchip is a bit much but dealing with Mimi anything could happen. Joie is my life and Mimi knows that. I'm not saying Mimi would ever hurt Joie but she might take her to hurt me. My job is to protect my sweet Joie's innocent from Mimi and anyone that looks like her. I walked out of the court building with my hat handed to me in on hand and a court day for a week later in the other hand. Of course I check the GPS chip reading to see if Sharon was telling the truth. My eyes wants to lie to my brain and say Sharon was wrong but she was accurate down to date and time. I can't wait to catch up to Mimi. The court put a time sensitive situation on finding Mimi. I climb back into my car with mix feelings and cut my phone off before I turned my car on. I didn't want Chuck GPSing me today through my phone. I let my frustration out on the steering wheel by heavily pounding my fist on it. I inhale deep. The new car smell is calming. I push my foot down on the gas with determination, heading straight to Harlem. I'm on the clock with seven hours to try to find Mimi's spiteful body and beat Chuck back home. I'm on my way to Free's public housing apartment. Free was a transfer student, meaning she ending up at the same high school as me and Mimi. She entered our high school in the middle of the second semester, freshman year. Free's a combination of revolutionary, ratchet and righteous which strengthen her fearlessness. She can verbally assault with educated Black Panther jargon but wasn't above ignorantly getting her hands dirty. Mimi was instantly captivated when Free vocally check the director of the school's History department. I was infatuated with her knowledge. I'm the studious one but Free would always surprise me with historical facts. She could be petty with her Black Panther jargon. If one of us didn't want to study, she would say "Did you know how many of your ancestors had to die so we could hold a book, much less have free will to read a book?" On a daily she pointed out things we took for granted. She reminded us of the sacrifices made so we could live with somewhat free will. She will use all her breathe until her last breathe to complain about the conditions in the public housing slash working poor complex but would never leave. She called it many things but it's her home. I don't think the community would let her leave she is the voice of the silent people. She created "Free Warriors" a group of people who mostly agree with Free and wanted better for the urban communities. She's the leader with the loudest voice protesting against injustice on City Hall's step. I started feeling all warm inside. I really missed the gang. We all looked alike. We all connected by the fact that we all was born May 21st same year in different places. I had spent the last eight years being a mother to Joie and a wife to Chuck that I completely forget about me. When I made the right turn off of Convent Avenue onto 129th I immediately felt like a teenager all over again. I'm hype inside to see Free. I know she would be hanging outside into middle of a dice game, swindling the players out their money. Many things change but habit is in every human. It's like magnetism. Free's energy is pulling me towards her. I recognize her curly afro standing out of the crowd in the park on St Nicholas Terrace. She has a red bandana tied around her head holding a single cigarette to her forehead, a clear sign she's on Rambo mood, looking for first blood. Clearly she's controlling the game. She bounce up in the other players faces shouting, waving her arms and pointing her fingers at the set of three dice on the gray cement. Her cut off black hoodie hula hooping around her waist as she search her thousand pockets on her black Army's Combat Uniform pants. She stomp her black suede construction boots in praise of her wins. With the money snatched up of the ground in one hand and a Corona® in the other hand Free perform her happy dance. She sat down on the bench to count out her winning in the face of the losing players. As soon as our eyes made contact she jump up off the bench and held her arms up in the air. I ran toward her. The happiness of seeing my friend had tears rolling down my cheeks. Free is the strongest of us all but even she couldn't hide her sniffles. Free's ears beg to hear me tell her about my life, play by play from the last time we saw each other eight years ago. She wanted to know all about Joie. Joie is now seven years old. She was in the second grade. She loves school, into the arts and loves to bake. I guess she picked up the drawing from me cause I love to doodle. She loves dancing. I wanted to show her pictures of Joie adorable gap tooth smile but I couldn't turn my phone on. I told Free about Chuck. Free couldn't believe I've been married for five years. Free ask did Mimi know about Chuck. I had to confess I haven't seen anybody other than Mimi since that night, in Brentwood. The night we promised to walk away from each other and never look back. The thought of that night makes the hairs on my neck stand up. I have relived that night over a hundred times. Waking up in the middle of the night in a cold sweat. My doctor prescribed me pills to settle my nervous so I could sleep through the night. I haven't been taking them often cause the nightmares have become rare lately. Free has been being free for the past eight years. I told Free about Dom and the subpoena. Free wasn't surprise by Dom's trying to get to Mimi through me. Dom is unpredictable like that. Everybody knew Mimi pulled the strings on Dom's brain but then out of nowhere he thinks for himself. It usually isn't a good thought but nonetheless it be his own. Free didn't know exactly where Mimi was but she was more than willing to help me find her. The next stop was Tricia's apartment which is near the Polo Grounds. I hop behind the wheel and Free hops into the passenger seat. Free removed her blood thirsty bandana, pulled her afro back tied it with a rubber band off her right waist and put on her righteous black beanie on. Tricia was abducted into Mimi's circle the end of our high school junior year. Tricia had come to our high school to finish her last year. She left her school because of being bullied. Tricia was bullied for the same reason she caught Mimi's attention, her clothes. Tricia was addicted to retail. She had five shoplifting arrest to prove she was a stone cold junkie. She always carries an extra outfit in her bag and was known to change at any given moment. I personal didn't like Tricia. She's fake. She was always attached to some drama, then bat her innocent eyes like she's the victim. She is a thief, a scammer and just plain mean. She always looked good with her make-up and all that designer fabric but she said the ugliest things. But Mimi hand-picked her and I trust Mimi judgment. I just side eye watch her. She wasn't home. We jump back into my car. Tricia should be on 125th getting her sticky fingers dirty. We drove across 125th street two times. On the third drive by Free spots Tricia coming out of the MAC store. First we drove along side of her beeping the horn trying to get her attention. But she is so stuck up she refused to look our way. She finally noticed it was us and not some thirsty guys trying to holler at her. I pulled over and we jump out of the car. I really didn't like Tricia but I did miss her. Tricia is like the annoying cousin close enough to be a sister. It's a love hate relationship but one thing is guaranteed she has my back and I have hers. After Free greeted her with hugs and kisses I was next in line. Seeing her was like being warped back to my teenage years. Under her foundation, eye shadow and lip stick it was like look at version of myself. We shared similar facial features. She had a cutie waist line Gucci® leather jacket with the signature stripes tied into a bow at the neck. Her hair is bone straight with a middle part. Tricia hops in the back seat of car. She hadn't heard from Mimi either. I filled her in on the past events. I told her about Dom subpoena and the time sensitive issue that came along with it. We decided to go to Shug's apartment on 105th and First Avenue. I took the FDR straight down. Tricia was catching me and Free up on her past eight years. When Tricia talk I count in my mind how many times she say "me." besides "me" being said twenty six times in five minutes, I found out she is sexing an eighteen year old. Excuse me he turns nineteen in two weeks. It smells like puppy love with a side order of DRAMA, Tricia's middle name. I couldn't help but notice she compared the nineteen year old to Lippa twice. Tricia opened her Jacket and through the rear view mirror I can see the scar around her neck from eight years ago. I remember that day like it was yesterday. It was the day that led to Brentwood and us losing contact. Tricia had introduced Mimi's circle to Erica Patterson and Nicole Grant from her old high school. They turned out to be snakes and because Tricia bought them to Mimi's circle Tricia had to pay. Mimi choked Tricia with an Iphone charger wire. I literally saw Tricia's eyes roll back in her head and her body went numb. It took all of us, me, Free and

Dom to get Mimi off Tricia. Mimi had forgiven Tricia but neither one of them will ever forget. The vibe between them was different. We roll up to Shug's building. Shug is a seventy-eight years old woman with a fifty-eight year old man. Shug lives like she is eighteen years old. She smoke marijuana and drink alcohol. And she ain't stingy. She has an open door policy, everyone is welcome. I remember the first time Mimi brought me to Shug's house. I couldn't believe my eyes. It was a senior citizen with Jordan's on her feet and premium weave on her head. And the double scoop of icing on the cake is her man twenty years younger than her. He in the background proudly claiming his Bae. Shug was my idol. I want to be old feeling young enjoying life. Free said if Mimi was around she had to stop by Shug's. It was like a hood rule. Please believe if Shug heard you was around and didn't check her, you'll hear about it. Free was right Mimi had spent a night at Shug's but left before Shug woke up. Dom has been sending letters to Shug's house for Mimi from jail. Mimi left the letters behind. I took them with me for safe keeping. Mimi could be anywhere by now that was hours ago. Free said the only other definite is Mimi favorite bar on Seventh Avenue but it was too early. The plan was to meet back up around eight-ish. I agreed but I didn't know how I was going to get around Chuck and Tricia reminds me of that fact. Tricia also felt the need to voice her opinions. Tricia's judgment's rubs me the wrong way. She believes Mimi would have a problem with me marrying into the blue shield.

"Stop worrying about my man and get a man!" My words was a stab at Lippa in Tricia's heart. As soon as I said the words I wanted to take it back. My words had gut punched her. She had loss the love of her life seven years ago and by the look on her face I could tell she truly hadn't gotten over him. she rolled her eyes at the back of my head with her immature attitude and mouth the word "bitch" and stuck out her tongue. I read her lip and saw her movements through the rearview mirror.

"Free, you going to sit there with pro-black beanie on and act like "Chuck" is grrreeaat choice?" Tricia questioned Free including the Tony the tiger arm gesture but her words were aimed at me.

"Don't come at my beanie, queen want to bee! Well since you asked my opinion, after Michael Brown, Trayvon Martin and Eric Garner just to list a few of many black man gunned down like dogs in street by the blue shield. The same shield that was put on the chest of slave hunters hundreds of years ago. So marrying a man wearing the shield is like Harriet Tubman marrying a white man. It's asinine!"

"Damn, Miss Farrakhan calm down! Sheeeeh! So him being white don't bother you, SISTER?" Tricia laughed as she egged Free on.

"See my uneducated SISTER, I don't have a problem with Caucasians because I know my history. And I'm going to learns you right now. The first human remains were discovered in Africa. And since the beginning of time black people have been able to reproduce albinos. Albinos are sensitive to sunlight. So the African people travel north of Africa to the Caucasus Mountains for the safety of the albinos. The other catered to the albinos while they were protected in the mountains. Over time their name changed from albinos to Caucasians, named after the mountain. So I could never have hatred toward by brothers and sisters."

"Ugh! I asked a simple yes or no question and professor X went in. Well I hope you prepared to give that same lesson to Mimi cause she ain't going to like the fact she married a white boy cop."

"I'm a great judge of character. I'll know if he good people once I meet him."

"That's never going to happen. I just want to put this behind us." I had to butt in and say something. I hated when they talked over me like I'm wasn't there. I would never subject Chuck to Mimi.

"So what's your plan perfect patty? We clear this up and split up again?" Tricia questioned more with her twisting neck than with her words.

"I didn't say all that."

"Cause you know the rules, outsiders are voted in!"

Tricia's words recovered memory from the buried high school files. It was freshman year I had won the school's science fair with my science partner Emilio Ramirez. I've won many awards before but this one was special cause I won it with Milio. I was completely intrigued by Milio's brain. He was like a human computer. He was packed with information, he was like a human google. He can compute any mathematical problem. Yes he was socially awkward. And he was far from a fashionesta. His dress code consist of maybe three pair of worn to torn jeans and plenty of worn tee shirts reping rock bands from the 70's. But he was kind to me and put my feeling above his own. I liked him but he wasn't voted in. I cried, begged and even try to bribe Mimi with money. But "RULES ARE RULES" and just like that Milio wasn't my friend anymore. He became Mimi daily target. She found humor in his humiliation. I'm just as guilty as she is cause I stood by with pain in my heart for him and watched. I didn't have the courage to stop her. I'm still remorseful for how I treated my friend Milio. My foot stomped on the brakes in a symbolic halt on Mimi's collision in my life. I'm in control.

"Damn! You did that on purpose! Don't hate me cause you ain't me." I completely ignored Tricia complaining. I made her draw outside her lips with her lipstick, big deal.

"We aren't in high school! There will be no voting on Chuck!"

"Rules are rules." Free words clearly stated she agreed with Tricia's adolescent policies.

"Free, eyes forward I'm changing my shirt."

"Gurl please! You ain't my type you too needy."

"Needy? Am not."

"Are too."

"I'm not and you not my type either, you never comb that afro and you dress style is boring with all that black."

"Are too."

"Children!" I had to disturbed the bickering my head was starting to hurt."

"Grandma keep your 4 eyes on the road, where's your glasses?" Tricia joked. I turned my glasses in for contacts years ago.

"Are you kissing yourself back there?" Free questioning the sound of smooches coming from the back seat. I had to laugh. Tricia is crazy about herself.

"I can't help myself, I'm just so dawn cute."

"Get over yourself." Free words was thrown over her shoulder with her face twisted in disgust.

"Get on yourself with that beat up beanie, here's $20, I'm sponsoring a new one. How are going to ever find someone, if don't dress up the package?"

"FYI! I'm seeing someone and she likes me just the way I am."

"She blind?"

"By love"

"Enough, I can't think straight! Please children!"

"Oh please Granny, loosen up just a bit, or do you know how? How you satisfying that husband?"

I dropped Tricia off first without an answer to her questions. I had enough of her popping that damn gum and her negative childish attitude. Then I dropped Free off. My head was hurting from Free's Black Panther jargon, Tricia self-centered vocals on top of them bickering. It was like a flash back to high school. Free had no shame in her game. At a drop of a dime she start preaching Black Panther jargon, in stores, restaurants or on the street. I can remember at least three times she's been arrested for disturbing the peace with her mouth. Oh, did I mention she occasionally walked with a bullhorn around her neck. She was even arrested for throwing red paint on a woman's mink in the name of animal rights. Numerous arrest for chaining herself to trees in attempt to stop demolition on urban public parks. She believe the lack of parks take away from human nature. Parks provides a place for exercises and oxygen is feed to air from the trees. With the city building residences on the playgrounds it is a major cause of an increase in obesity and asthma in urban children. Thank god, Tricia wasn't in the mood to just aggravate Free by eating a hot dog or burger in front of Free's vegan eyes. It drives Free insane. The combination of Free and Tricia together without the referee, Mimi was a lot at one time. I headed back to Riverdale. On the drive I was wondering what Dom's simple brain was thinking. Ok, by some miracle the court give him the right to see Joie, then what? You scare the poor child with you six foot five inches of disproportion weight. I really didn't know Dom personal. We been in each other's company be we never exchange more than two words with one other. He usually ask "Gege, U good?" and I would nod yes. That was our relationship. I knew in my heart that if I was ever "not good" Dom would take care of it. But I never used the Dom card. I could never understand Mimi and Dom's relationship. It was so imbalance. Either they were love birds hugging, kissing and touching or they were fighting to the death. Once time at Dom's mother house they got into a big fight. Mimi intentionally slammed his hand in the door, repeatedly. His pinky, ring and middle finger were broken on his right hand. She then sat with him four hours in the emergency room while his fingers were reset and doctors casted his fingers. I tell you every moment with Mimi is adventure. Mimi had the power to bring out the very best or the very worst in a person. I don't know how she does it but in seconds she is controlling a room filled of people. I arrive to Riverdale right on schedule. With enough time to start dinner, go pick up Joie from school and drop of her off at dance, go back home finish dinner and then pick Joie up from dance all before Chuck comes home. As soon as I enter Riverdale's boarders I turn my phone on...I texted Chuck a picture of the court papers with a nice text message, "I'm working on putting the past behind me. I need you trust me, loving you always"

THREE

I'm in a great mood besides the fact of me ducking Chuck for four days. He wanted to talk about the court date but I still haven't talk to Mimi. I need to talk to her before I talk to Chuck. I feel like tonight is the night I'm going finally catch up with Mimi and slow down for Chuck. It was easier than I thought it would be or was Chuck avoiding me? I took another "me" day. I left the flower shop in Amy's hands. Orders ready to be delivered. They are wrapped, loaded and ready to go with Dickey. Dickey, born Richard Wright, an oddly lanky adorable freckled faced, eighteen year old kid that occasionally delivers for the shop. I had brunch pool side of Riverdale's up scaled spa. I indulged in a deep tissue massage and a steam bath. I ended the day with a little shopping therapy before returning to the condo. I sashayed into the lobby feeling refreshed and confident about facing my monster in the closet, Mimi.

Norman the doorman greets me with a "Good Afternoon, Mrs. Irwin."

His words hit my ears and jolted a skip in my step. I jerk my body to face him. I was so tuned into my thoughts that nothing around me had volume. After five years it still shocks me when I'm referred to as Mrs. Irwin. Mrs. Irwin is Chuck's mother. Don't misinterpret my words. Mrs. Irwin is a sweet woman. She's just not sweet to me. She felt like her son was marrying under his class. She had her eyes and heart set on Ashley Collon since Chuck was in middle school. And since I entered into the picture with a one year old, Joie, I really don't fit into Mrs. Irwin's mold. She's very unapologetic disrespectful to our marriage. She invited Ashley to every family gathering as her personal plus one. Ashley accepts each offer extended to her but never over step, in fact she made a conscious effect to extra nice to me. but I know a snake when I see one. I checked my watch on the elevator's ride up. I'm keeping an eye on every seconds. It's confirmed there's more than enough time to start dinner. Unitizing my spare minutes to stop by the supermarket to pick up a few things. I stuck my key into the lock of the condo's front door. Before I could put my supermarket bags down on the floor Chuck grabs me up off my feet and pin my back to the wall in front of the plank stairs by his strong grip on my raincoat collar. I try to explain that I was coming from the supermarket.

"I know when you in the house, at the shop or when you just cruising around spend money. Just cause I'm working all the time don't think I don't know what's going on around here. You can't say I don't let you breathe. Spend extra G's on your flower shop so you can pursue your dream. Do you remember the brand new 2015 SUV with the custom license plates? 5 years later I'm still paying for ice freezing your finger. Last month we made hot steamy love in the West Indies. I think about our love when I hold you. But I see my love is easy for you to abuse and in your eyes there isn't any remorse. But I can't stop loving you no matter how much I try..."

As his words fall from his lips they land on my heart. His glassy eyes and soften loosen his hold on my collar. I stare into his eyes and feel his heart. I try to speak but the fear of my words made him grip my face. His thump on the left side of my face and his four fingers on the right side of my face. The pressure of his right hand is crushing my cheeks. He place his lips on top of my duck lips. His right hand release my face and I'm allowed to kiss him back. He parts his lips and his tongue enters my mouth. My tongue tango with his tongue as the palm of his right hand caress the left side of my face. He breaks away from my lips and without hesitation he extend his right arm, wraps his right hand around my throat.

"Somebody said they saw you in Harlem today, last week you was spotted in the Bronx and the person you were kissing wasn't me. I know that you are creeping the disrespect is that you let it show. You should've respected my house and just kept it to yourself. I would never ask you cause I don't want to know. I don't usually watch your whereabouts but it how you moving. You can't deny it something is off. When looking in your eyes, I don't want to believe it. I'm not applying no pressure but I have to know do you want to stay or go cause my heart can't take it anymore."

I had opened my mouth to tell him my answer but first I wanted to tell him I wasn't creeping.

"Don't even try it, I know when your lying."

Lying? It's funny how I'm under a microscope with spys included but he walks in and out of the condo at any giving time. And let's not get into them damn scratches on his back. I have yet to mention the fact he wakes up daily to a woman's voice mail. Tears started rolling down my cheeks not because I was lying but because I was being questioned. Questioned like a suspect again. I was crying because he would never understand the friendship between me and Mimi. To explain Dom I had to start with Mimi.

"Don't even do that, I know why you crying."

With all my heart I want to tell him everything from the very beginning, the day I met Mimi to precise end, that night in Brentwood. Holding my past from him was hurting me just as much as it was hurting him. I palm his face with both of my hands and plant a thousand kisses on his expression of doubt. Everything is deeper than the surface. I truly did love Chuck. Chuck showed me what love is. This was just one of those things I had to take care of by myself for myself. Would he really understand I dream of angels and live with demons?

"Being married means we are a team. We handle problems together. I have plenty of recourses that can be helpful. I want to help you with whatever it is."

The problem begun before his time. It's a delicate matter and has to be approached in a subtle way. Having Riverdale police beating down door and questioning people isn't going to get no answers. And it's a proven fact it's not very effective.

"I don't want to let you go but you have to let me in. I'm not prepared to let you throw away five years but I'm not willing to fight for someone I've already lost."

Chuck words wet with anguish. But I try to paint the light at the end of the tunnel.

We could make it through this. Our love is strong enough to withstand any storm. I wasn't just saying words to distract Chuck from the "Dom" conversation, I meant every word. He could read my truth in my heart. He kiss me on my forehead, down my nose landing his lips on top of my lips. The sensation in his lips said words he didn't speak. His love was outlined as his hands traced my flesh. My father use to say "A woman can always tell how much a man loves her by his kiss". His lips are tender filled with salvia dripping with affection, outlining his love by repeating "I love you." At that moment our love was stronger than the scratches on his back, sturdier than Dom's subpoena. Our love is pure. Through Chuck's glassy eyes I heard him. A thousand kisses from his butter soft lips is never too much. He holds me tight and close to his body. His love swept me off my feet and carried me up the plank stairs to our bedroom. He gently laid me down on the bed. Eye to eye I could see his pure soul. His soft skin covering my body set my mind at ease. He passionately strokes packed with intense love. No words spoken. We have had sex plenty of times but this time our soul connected. The feeling of love is more powerful and far deeper than it has ever been. My head hit the pillow and I was floating in the skyline outside the wall windows. I'm fighting a losing battle against sexitis as the lights on the bridge tinkle in my eyes...

***

Watching Gege fall asleep in my arms is the most comforting feeling in the world. I can't help myself but stare at her chest rise and fall from breathing. Her beauty is enchanted. She has an angelic face with wicked eyes. There's a long story behind her eyes but I can't read it. I kiss her face several times as she slept. Her stillness make her so appealing. I sneaked in one last kiss before going to pick Joie up from dance class. I asked the master chef, Joie what should we cook for dinner. "Homemade pizza rolls" was Joie's dinner idea. I just listened and drove as Joie verbally listed and wrote down the ingredients. I'm always hypnotized by Joie mature vocabulary and knowledge. In the supermarket Joie picked up the items off her list, four pack of Pilsbury biscuit tubes, two bags of sliced pepperoni and two bags of shredded mozzarella cheese. I just paid at the register Joie did all the work. On the ride from the supermarket to the condo Joie filled my ears with the events of her day. We both greet Norman the doorman on the way in. Norman always have a little magic trick for the children of the building. Today's magic trick is pulling a oversize chocolate quarter out from behind Joie's ear. I play more amazed than Joie, she just half smiled at Norman. Joie throw the chocolate quarter into the elevator garbage.

"Why did you throwing it out?"

"Bad man give candy to little girls to gain trust and when you trust bad man bad thing happen."

Joie's words hit stronger than a swift kick to the throat. "Who told you that?"

"It's call stranger danger, Mimi told me bout it, at school."

I let Joie turn the key to open the front door to the condo. I went to check on Gege. I wanted to invite her helping hands into the kitchen to cook dinner with myself and Joie. To my surprise, she was still sleeping like a sweet angel. I stole a kiss off her forehead before return my full attention to sweet Joie. I wash my hands as commanded by Chef Joie. She had already washed her hands and put on her little adorable apron. I'll tell on myself because I know Joie won't leave out, so yes, I used Gege's apron. The sight of me in the apron made Joie laugh so hard her legs gave way and she was wiggling on the floor. She try her best to return her focus back to preparing dinner with small hiccups spells of giggles every now and there. She had line the kitchen island with all the groceries bought from the supermarket. She is prepared to start dinner some adults aren't as organized as Joie. I stood in awe. Her little seven year old body gracefully dance in the kitchen like a grown woman. Joie instructed me to turn on the oven to three hundred twenty five degrees. She sucked her teeth at that the fact she had to tell me. I didn't have fancy foot work in the kitchen. Joie wasn't old enough or strong enough to work the electric can opener. It's my job to open the can of tomato sauce. I dumped the sauce into the bowl like the boss said. As she yell out spices salt, pepper, garlic, and oregano, I took them out the cabinet and pass them to her, only because she's too short to reach. She used a she sprinkle of each and then pass each one back. She said "Cleaning while you cook is the best way not to end up with a big mess." I just shook my head in agreeance. I was ordered to open a tube of biscuts. We both almost jumped out of our skin at the sound of the tube popping open. We shared a chuckle at each other's silliness. She reached into the refrigerator and took out a bottle of honey bar-b-que sauce. "Some people put sugar in tomato sauce to sweeten it I like this better." She answered the puzzled look on my face. She added a spoonful of honey bar-b-que sauce into the tomato sauce and stirred. She then handed the bowl of sauce mix and instructed that I place it in the microwave for one minute and a half. Before I could finish my task she was already kneed the biscuits dough down into flat circles. I volunteered to assist. She laughed at my kneed technique. I then remove the sauce from the microwave "with the oven mitten on" like the boss ordered. I placed the hot bowl on the kitchen island. She stirred the sauce before blowing a spoon fill of sauce before taste testing it. Her pleased expression made me beg for a sample taste of sauce. It was really good, no I mean damn good. I'm impressed. She then topped the circle dough with a spoonful of sauce mix in a circular motion, next sliced pepperoni and shredded mozzarella. She then rolled the dough up into a cylinder shape. "You have to pinch the sides, so the sauce don't come out." Joie asked me for the cookie sheet pan. I was her adult robot that she complete control. She than buttered the pan. I just stood there mesmerized. My eyes are wondering how many seven years was able to do what Joie can do. I helped her place the dough rolls on the sheet pan. We put on our oven mittens and put the pan of homemade pizza rolls in the oven. She set the timer for 25 minutes. We washed our hands over a little playful water fight. She immediately pull out homework and started sounding out the instructions. But kept a close eye on the clock. Joie had a cut a paste assignment. Joie read the instructions out loud. She then followed the instructions. She studied her spelling words. She had eight of the ten words down pack. By the time she was finished with her homework the pizza rolls were done. We mitten up and removed the pan of pizza roll with a mouthwatering aroma streaming into our nose from the oven. Joie begged me with giggles in her voice for me to take off the apron. I entertained Joie with jokes as she intrigued me with her mannerisms. Joie giggled at my every move. After dinner it was her bedtime, eight pm. But I allowed her to stay up pass her bedtime to watch her favorite show Master Chef. We munched down some cookies, popcorn and ice cream which was also a "no no". She said "For a cop you break a lot of rules." I had to laugh. Joie laughed herself right to sleep on the couch under my arm. Within minutes my eyelids were getting heavy the television screen was getting smaller and smaller...

***

I jumped up out of my sleep. I was so mad at myself for letting Chuck rock me to sleep. I planned on calling Free and Tricia to apologize for completely missing the met up again. I was hoping that at least they finally caught up to Mimi. But first I had to check on Joie. I peeped in on the TV watching Joie and Chuck in the living from the hallway. I love that Chuck accepted Joie from day one. Never once treating her less than his own. Watching them bonding warmed my heart. I went back to my bedroom. I texted the girls in a group text to see if Mimi showed up to the bar, on Seventh Avenue. No she didn't but she was spotted in the Bronx, on 167th street off of Jerome Avenue. Of course when they arrived to the bar they had just missed her. The bartender, claims she saw Mimi in the bar every night at around seven-ish for the past last two weeks. Free chimed in to mention the bartender name in Kelly. Kelly revealed that Mimi always comes alone and changes her clothes in restroom. Kelly even remembered what drink Mimi had and how many, four shots of vodka and left with the same guy each time. "The Guy" is a big and scary guy. I could depend on Free to fondle all the details out of Kelly. Free had a way with woman. Kelly also remember that today Mimi paid with a credit card when she usually pays with cash. Kelly was very generous to Free's flirtatious grin and found the receipt. My eyes almost fell out of my head when I saw the picture of the receipt with my name clearly printed under the signature line. The nerve of Mimi to keep using my name without my knowledge or permission. In high school I was Miss Goodie. I never was in any trouble. Ms. White the assistant principal was a personal friend of my deceased mother. Ms. White always looked out for me, turning the other way when trouble was in my way. So when Mimi, Free and Tricia used my name in school the offence was sweep under the rug. But we are adults now and using my name is unacceptable. I really had to find Mimi. This is the final step. I'm feeling type way about her sneaking Joie to a penitentiary, exposing her young impressionable eyes to the darkness of a jail. Now using my name is just too far. I have never stood up to Mimi. I've accepted all her decisions good, bad and ugly without saying a word but I'm not that timid teenage I'm an adult who makes my choices. Free left her number behind with Kelly. Kelly promised to call Free when Mimi is sighted again. But I'm sure Kelly will be calling before then. I checked up on Joie and Chuck again. Joie was fast asleep under Chuck's left armpit, his arm cradling her little body. I couldn't fall back to sleep. Out of pure curiosity I started reading Dom's letters to Mimi from jail. It wasn't an evasion of privacy, she is running around town using my name on a fake card. She is playing a dangerous game I'm the wife of police officer. We have shared everything with each other, or so I thought. There were mostly, birthday cards addressed to all four of us, Birthday cards for Joie, Valentine's Day cards, Thanks Giving cards and Christmas cards for each year of Dom's incarceration. There were two four page letters. The first one was from the beginning of his sentences. Most of the letters were filled with words remising about the past. Dom always was around but he was so quite I often forgot he was in the room with us. We never had a full conversation but I would say we went out his way to be a gentlemen to me, Free and Tricia. Though the years Dom would always gave us all Valentine's Day, Birthday and Christmas gifts along with Mimi, of course Mimi gift were bigger and better but he still though of us. And for that I had a special place in my heart for Dom. Reading his memories reminded me of our unspoken bond. Dom helped Free "clean out her closet." As Free's closest friends we know she was into girls she didn't have to tell us. Especially after her "romantic little thing" with Erica Patterson. But it made her feel better by saying the words in the air. Dom had spent seven years of his life in jail for Tricia's drama. Tricia is nothing but drama. Brentwood is all on Tricia. The letters were written like Dom knew we all were going to read them. But some letters were just for Mimi cause it was written on a separate paper.

To my love,

Please don't be mad at me I know you said no letters just cards but I miss you more than anything. Your face is the last thing I see before I go to sleep and the first thing I see in the morning. I spend my days dreaming of Joie's little face. And you holding her little body in your arms. Although we are miles apart I can still feel y'all energy. Tell Tricia to stay out of drama. And I hope Free don't become a political prisoner. I know you not going to like what I write next but you should listen to Gege scary ass, sometimes her precautious nature will say you a lot of time. And please try you best to contain you rage.

Love always,

Dom

The second letter to Mimi:

My love I be home very soon. I can't wait to see everybody especially Joie. My 1st night home I want to take everybody to eat at our favorite spot.

See you soon

Dom

After reading the letters I realized just how sweet Dom's heart really is. Dom is the perfect example of not judging a book by its cover. Dom is a gentle giant with a big loving heart. As I scan the letters and cards for any clues left behind that will lead to finding Mimi. "Favorite spot"... Every birthday from sixteen years old to eighteen we celebrated the day on Staten Italy. Once the reservation included a yacht ride from downtown Manhattan straight to the dock behind the restaurant. The ride only isn't the only thing that set this restaurant above any other Italian restaurant, the food was hand cook by authentic Italian woman. A mom and pop little Italian restaurant with big favor. Stepping off the yacht and into the restaurant was like leaving New York and walking across the Atlantic Ocean floating into the Mediterranean Sea right to Italy. Its amazing indoor outdoor dining area is to die for. On the left and right side are buildings with Venetian windows looking down on the table and chairs. Under my feet is overseas cobblestone flooring illuminated with ten feet tall Italian lamp post capturing Italy's scenery. The fresh baked bread consumed the air and the homemade pasta filled my stomach and warmed my heart. Even the plate had the Italy curved lines embedded in the ceramic pieces of art. I decide to wait until tomorrow evening to visit the restaurant to see if Dom and Mimi had been there recently. The owner Vinny was like an uncle to Dom. Vinny is a retried correctional officer. Vinny first meet Dom on the job at Juvenile detention center. Dom was a frequent visitor so they built a relationship that extended beyond the gate. I hope Vinny remembers me when I get there. Just as I was about to give up on searching for any other clues. I received a text. It was from Dom, "Flower shop in 20 minutes-Dom" I walked on my toes out of the condo. My heart sunk into my stomach once I was outside the condo door. I felt so guilty sneaking out after midnight but I had some questions for Dom. I flew out the building with my night grown blowing in the wind. I use my right hand to hold my raincoat closed over my silk night grown. The slippers on my feet made me glide across the lobby's waxed floor out the door right to my parked car outside the building. With my foot on the gas my mind is racing. The flower shop is a dream that Chuck made come true for me. Chuck is so good to me my heart is breaking for having to keep him at a distance from Mimi. I fell in love with flowers from my scribble scrabble. When my mind travel with a pencil in my hand magic happens. Drawing paths that creates floral images with hidden words appears. Who would guess my hand's art would earned me a scholarship into Columbia University. Drawing floral designs was just a hobby that turned in to a true love of flowers and plants. It was amazing to me how one little seed could blossom into an incredible intersex beauty. It's marvelous that a flower can have both sex organs and never forced to choose. Each growing into all shapes, color and sizes, all the same but all so different. The end result is something beautiful and unique, all stemming from a small little nothing seed. I reached the flower shop in record time. I really didn't have long I needed to be back home before Chuck woke from his nap and notice I had left. That was another issue I didn't want to create. Dom had five minutes. My body shook with nervousness. My hand jiggled with the keys before opening the front doors to the flower shop, the French doors opens outward. During operating hours I hold the doors open with to large flower pots, sprouting Morning Glory greetings. The flower shop is on prime real estate sitting in the center of Main street. In walking distance from the flower shop is Riverdale's church, hospital, school and largest office building in the zip code. The right and left wall of the flower shop are sliding door refrigerators filled with all types of flavorsome flowers. The dim illuminated fridge accentuated the dainty curves and elegant posture of each flower. The right side fridge accommodates fifty different variation of the unforgettable rose. Of course my favorite is Moscow's September of 2010 gold medal winner the GIGI. The exclusive medium warm pink rose is a winner in every sense. The stunning color is just like myself calm yet intriguing like there's more under the first set of petals. The different colored roses glowed in my eyes like eyes candy on a store's counter. Some roses were so sweet I could take a bite out of them. The yummy sugary delights of the gold strike rose shines lemon head bright yellow. The sweet bazooka pink Geraldine bubble with flavor. The chickco stick orange Free spirit rose is eye watering. The edge of white base blush rose appeared to be painted with lipstick candy. I have to laugh at my own guilt of making my juvenile lips sticky and red pretending to be wearing candy based lipstick. In the left fridge are the imported French flowers. Dickey has a standard six am pick up on Tuesdays and on Thursdays at the airport. French flowers are full of flavor with unique arches and personality. The dignitary Ranunculus flower with many noble orange layers. The media magnet, Stargazer lily draws attention with wild purple petals dancing around the star center. Hydrangeas scream at all eyes with the big fluffy personality coming in many different mood shades. Amaryllis is a common upper class house hold guest complements to its red star shine. With the light off the glow in fridge make the flowers come to life. In front of the fridges are two story stands of me and Amy's homegrown herbs and potted plants. My flower shop is a slice of heaven packed into four walls. During the day the shop is beautiful. The flowers strutting their best in sun but at night the shop came alive. The moon light rays shined through glass roof down onto the flowers. The flowers looked as if they were coated with sliver glitter, glowing like Disney© princess cut diamonds. The Pink cherry blossoms branches draped like sprinkling Christmas lights. Upon entering the shop I pushed the code into the alarm system, the last thing I need was for Riverdale finest to show up. When I turn around the beauty of the shop had snuck up on me and I just stood in awe at the amazing gorgeousness. Caring for them all is a job bigger than me. Thank goodness of the heavens for Amy. She loves flowers just as much as me. She cared for them like they were her children. She gave each flower and plant the individual attention they deserved. I walk toward the back wall where my station is at. It's a multipurpose area. I wrap arrangements, take payments and freshen up flowers and plants all on that wooden table. Behind the table the store's phone is mounted on the wall. I saw a large shadow moving around in the back. Before I could get a better look. Dom jumped out and I jumped out of my skin. I stumbling backwards knocking over potted plants off the stand. Doom reach out and grab on to my right arm, preventing me from falling on my back. Minutes after I had caught my breath my heart was still pounding, Dom had scared me to death popped out of the darkness. I cut my hand trying to pick up the shattered clay pot. On the right side of the wooden table is a sink. I went over to the sink to run cold water on my hand. I know it was a small cut but with the excessive bleeding I couldn't see where the blood was coming from. Dom walks over to the sink investigating my injury. Dom's size made me nervous. I know he would never harm me but I jumped from his presence anyway. He grab my hurt hand and squeezed my cut middle finger. I let out a small moan from the pain Dom was inflicting. To my surprise the bleeding had stop. I reached under the wooden table to get a band aid to seal the split. Dom wrapped the band aid around my finger. I caught the glimpse of his gentleness. "You good?" these are the first words Dom spoke. I had no time for catching up. I need straight answers.

"Why did you subpoena me for visitation of Joie?"

"Mimi made me to do that."

"Is everything ok in here?" Amy voice her concerns. She heard the clay pot shatter from upstairs. She came down from her studio apartment to check on things. I truly appreciate Amy. Her heart is pure. Our relationship is beyond employer and employee. Amy become my friend during my short stay at the hospital. After I was released we lost touch but when Mimi dump Joie in my lap, literally Amy was the only one there. The first year of Joie life was rough. Juggling college and a newborn isn't easy at all. At least Mimi had left me money to get by on. My father wasn't interested in having a baby in his home. I was alone, lost, young, with a college scholarship and a newborn on my arms. I used some of the money Mimi and Dom left me with to pay brokerage fee, security deposit and first month's rent for an apartment. Seventeen hundred secured a match box in a South Bronx tenement building. It was nothing to brag about but I was proud to have a home of my own. The little beat up, five floor walkup, studio apartment didn't have enough room to breathe. It was a tight fit for me and Joie, not to mention the squatters, the mice and roaches. Me and Joie shared a twin size mattress. Joie love was the only thing pulling me through this tough time. September came I hadn't established a child care for Joie so I couldn't attend class. I contacted the college to confirm my I had a spot for the following winter semester. I recall every time the phone on the other end rung in my ear my heart skipped a beat. Thank goodness my scholarship and my spot was going to be preserved until January. Even though the call went in my favor I still wasn't relieved, I didn't have a plan. But never once did I ever considered just hunting Mimi down and returning her offspring. Joie's unconditional love is the air I breathe, the blood flowing through my body keeping me alive. In November as me and Joie were leaving her six month check-up appointment we ran into Amy. We had years to catch up on. She offered to drive me and Joie home. I accepted with no hesitation. Traveling from bus and to trains with a baby and stroller is manual labor. Then to have the five floor walk-up waiting on me when finally get home made me sweat just thinking about. I had to ride in the back sit with Joie, Amy's 1997 Honda Civic wasn't equipped with a car seat. We stop and talked over coffee at a small mom and pop style dinner three blocks down from my building. It's really a hang out spot for retirees. Old people loves babies. Joie was no different while she was being entertained, I forced my attention to Amy. We gossiped about the past as we walked from the coffee shop to my building. Amy was there for me when I was in deep dark place where light couldn't reach. So I opened up to Amy about it all how Mimi had left me with her responsibility and now I was neglecting accountability for my life. I would literally die if Joie would have been taken from my arms but at the same time I felt like I was kicking the bucket of my dreams. Amy wiped my tears and wrapped her arms around me so tight it gave life to words, "I'm here." Since that day til this day Amy hasn't strayed from her words or my side. My mind jumped from Amy to Mimi. Mimi is known to handcraft facts and draw a nice clean picture around it, creating a believable story that's far from the truth. "It's not what you do, it's what you can prove!" is the words that come before the lie I would be forced to rememorize. I just couldn't see the artsy drawing she was building in front of me with the subpoena.

"I'm completely confused. Why would Mimi tell you to file for visitation? I have never kept either one of you away from y'all daughter. She didn't have to sneak Joie to see you! And I wanted to know why is she still using my damn name? Where is she?" I try to bite my tongue for Amy's ear sake but my tongue couldn't contain the words.

"I don't have the answers you looking for. Mimi sent me here to tell to get the girls together and met her at Pier 25 at 4pm tomorrow."

And just like that Dom walked out the front door. I wanted to jump into my car and follower his ass right to Mimi but Amy's facial expression solicited information. She had already overheard too much. Instead of supplying Amy with information I gave her an assignment to review all my credit cards statements online for questionable purchases. Nothing is sitting right with me. I just walked out of the shop leaving Amy to reset the security alarm and lock the door. Driving back to the condo I was more lost than before I came to meet Dom. Mimi is frustrating me with her games. I really wanted to know what's her plan? We weren't teenagers no more. Running New York City's streets without any responsibility isn't how I live anymore. The car ride home I could barely drive due to the butterflies swimming in my stomach. I didn't want to fight with Chuck over something I just couldn't explain. How could I begin to explain what I don't understand myself? I open the door to the condo hoping Chuck was still asleep. But when I open the door he was sitting in front of the kitchen island. I walked in and when our eyes meet, I looked like a deer caught in head lights. My mouth opened to offer him apologetic words for sneaking out of the condo. He stopped me from talking with his body language. He put his index finger over his lips and shook his head from side to side. Before the door could close behind me Chuck walk out with a look of disgust painted on his ora. I felt horrible for what I'm doing to Chuck, to us. I was going free our relationship from these secrets. After I see Mimi I'm going to tell Chuck everything.

***

Moments before Gege returned...
I carried Joie's sleeping body to her room and place her angelic body in her bed. I peeped into my bedroom to check on my loving wife, in hopes to steal another kiss. I wiped my eyes to make sure I wasn't seeing clearly and not sleep walking. The bed was empty. I'm baffled. I can't believe she would sneak out while I was napping. My mind is racing in different directions. Was she meeting up with Dom? I didn't know what to think. I just don't know who she is nowadays. Every time I confront her she proclaiming her love for me but is playing me for a fool? My whole job depends on the fact of being able to tell when someone is lying but yet with

Gege I just don't know. I called my partner Nathan Miller to track Gege whereabouts. Everything in my heart is leading me to Domonique Thomas. I stole Domonique's file from the police department once he served the subpoena. I had no other choice. Gege wouldn't even say his name. I want to know just who this man is. I really wanted to meet him face to face, man to man. But if I go near him I could lose everything but staying away from him is costing me my wife. I've read his jacket over hundred times. I know it like a pastor knows the Bible...

Domonique "Dom" Thomas...

D.O.B: February 12th, 1987
Age: 30 year old
Height: 6'5
Tattoo and/or scars: heart shaped tattoo with the broader as manes, Mimi, Gege, Free, Tricia on upper right arm. Who is Mimi, Free and Tricia? At this very moment I wondered if this "Mimi" and the "Mimi" that taught Joie about stranger danger is the same person? At ten years old Dom stabbed a fellow student with a mechanical pencil. The pencil punctured the skin, so he was charged in family

court and mandated counseling. He was then picked up a year later for shoplifting in a department store. Family court slapped him on the waist again with more counseling. Then the following year he beat a man's face in and robbed the battered man by taking his wallet and phone. Professional diagnosed him with emotional/mental illness. He spent some time in an institution that treat his condition. He was released with given more counseling and medication. One year after that, at the tender age of thirteen he was arrested for selling "Lady G, triple stacks" ecstasy pills on high school grounds. For this charge he stood in front of criminal court judge. The judge didn't stutter when she sentence him to Juvenile detention center until his eighteen birthday which equaled five years. He was released 6 months before his 18th birthday. For five years he manage to stay out of police contact. Then at twenty three years old he was arrested for beating Westley "Lippa" Gavin to death with his bare hands. He maxed out his seven years in upstate prison for Lippa's death. His prison money account remained filled the whole 7 years. Who was putting money in his account? His file clearly states he didn't have active parents. He bounced from foster home to group home never a home to call his own. So who was putting money on his books? Miller's sister still feels like justice wasn't served for her son's death. I don't know if the loss of her only son or the fact that she don't have full knowledge of the circumstances surrounding her son's death that was driving her insane. My eyes inhale the words off the pages and I exhaled disbelief MY sweet innocent Gemini was mixed up with a petty low level criminal like Dom. I can't comprehend Gemini playing me and keeping Dom a secret. What would she want with someone like Dom? I recognized Gege's name being a part of Dom's tattoo, she can't deny it. She doesn't spell "Gege" like everybody else. She down play the relationship between herself and Dom but when a man tattoo a woman's name on his skin its deeper than the eyes can see. But the name "Tricia" has been ringing in my head for weeks. I knew I've seen that name before. Where did I see that name? Then it hit me like a ton of bricks. Could I have stumbled across new evidences? Every police officer has caught a case that stay with them. Many years will pass but the freshness will never grow stale. I, Charles "Chuck" Irwin, is not exempt from the blue shield curse. My 1st homicide case as detective remains cold but hot in my heart. Two eighteen year old females named, Erica Patterson and Nicole Grant. Their bodies found in the wood area in Brentwood, LI, burnt to a crisp. We were only able to identify Erica by the char remaining's of her breast implants serial numbers. Nicole only recognized by the serial number in her artificial teeth. Three weeks before their bodies were found they had agreed to cooperate with the police to take down their boss. They had admitted their guilty participation. The whole scam revolved around a black box. The two girls were recruited because they held part-time jobs at Bloomingdales. Their duties were to swipe as many credit cards as they could through the black box for a thousand dollars a week. The black box then extract all information attached to the card, name address, birthday, social security numbers and pin number. The information is then transferred into creating new card. The program was more intelligent than a straight line from one account to another. I sat in the living room with the old case files spread across the floor waiting to see how long it will take Gege to be fucked by her lover. The alcohol is fueling my rage. I provide a good thing here for her and Joie. How could she betray me for a person like Dom? I started rereading each interview through the vodka glass. When I found the name Tricia in Veronika Patterson's statement. I shouted for joy. It was my only confirmation I wasn't completely crazy. Veronika Patterson is Erica Patterson mother. Veronika Patterson states that "Tricia" picked both Erica Patterson and Nicole Grant up from her apartment. She was positively sure because she invited the young girl in and gave her a drink of soda. Veronika even remembered Tricia walking out the door with both girls. She even remembered Nicole's wearing a brand new red motorcycle leather jacket cause she liked it for herself. Tricia was the last person to be seen with the two girls alive. I have searched the world for an eighteen year old named Tricia but never found that the girl even existed. But here is her name tattoo to Dom's arm. It can't be coincidence or could it be? I could hear my phone ringing in my head but my blur vision couldn't locate it. Finally I found it, it's my partner Miller. Just as I answered the phone Gege entered the condo. In a slightly tipsy movement I swiped up all the paper work that was scattered all over the place. I shuffled the papers into my office and locked the door behind me. I never once looked in Gege's direction but when I did, I wish I hadn't. I can't believe she was running the street in her negligée. Is that dirt on her slipper? Where did she go? I didn't want to question her or fuck fight her. I'm disgusted by her lies. I just staggered out the condo. I should arrest her ass for indecent exposure! Miller is parked in front of the building. I went down to vent to Miller's ears. Why am I feeling like the wife with a cheating husband, crying to anyone who willing listen? I had no shame in front of Miller. Miller is my partners and partners is always there. I sat in the passenger's seat of Miller's car. He shows me the pictures of Gege meeting with Dom at her flower shop just moment ago. The pictures didn't show them hugging or kissing but they were close together in the corner for more than a few seconds. What's going on with me?

I'm not the jealous type but I can feel it in every part of my body everything is tied into one. The fact that she sneaked to meet him, dressed in lingerie not only bothered me it was racking my brain. I'm hurt cause she's lying to me but her not being able to talk to me cut me deeper. My mind started asking questions "Did she show him all those things that she used to do to me." I wanted to question her but was afraid of her answers. I decided that moment that if she goes back to see him she can't come back to me. It's might be best if I left. My heart is bleeding through my eye. I had to tell Miller about Dom's connection to my cold case. Miller don't think Dom could be the key to close both of my problems but we did agreed Dom has earned himself a visit from Riverdale's finest.

"You already know neither one of us can go near him." Miller felt the need to voice his warning.

"I know that but this about my family... I want to know what he knows and I want to hear it from his mouth."

"And staying away from him is about my family... ok let's say you're right and the two cases are connected. You really think Domonique Thomas is going to just hand the final piece over to you?"

"I know he is! I can feel it in my bones! But how do we get close to fire without getting burnt?"

"I talked to Ashley. She's able to go place we can't. She found out he was put in a halfway house. 3 days in, 4 days out, trying to work him back into society. The program provides him with a cellphone with GPS tracking. I got a cellphone number..."

"Why didn't you say that from the start..."

"Once I give you the number I'm done. You will be on your own from here on out."

"You still holding on to the number." I'm so anxious to get my hands on that piece of paper.

"Look bro, It's a cold case from 7 years ago... you going to give up your life, your badge, all for a cold case? Is it really worth everything?"

"I see their torched bodies every time I close my eyes. I seen the hurt in the parent's eyes when I had no answers. And my heart is burning to know the truth about him and Gege."

"Here the number... I'm draw the line on any involvement. I'm telling you it just don't feel right."

"Fine drop me off at the nearest gas station, so I can make the call, time is ticking."

I didn't have a car of my own. I had to turn it in for route expectation, department policy. Miller drives to the nearest gas station and I jump out the car before the wheels come to a complete stop. I flew inside the store at the gas station, flashing my badge and demanding a phone. The poor cashier is so shaken like I holding the place up. He almost fell trying to get the phone to the counter. I'm so anxious I missed dialed two time, or maybe it's the effect of the alcohol. Finally after I focused my blur vision in on the phone then I was able to dial the right number. With a sense of accomplishment I stuffed the piece of paper with the number written on it into my left pants pocket. Each ring in my ear made my forehead sweat harder.

"Hello…"

"Domonique Thomas, I'm Charles …

"I know who you are."

"Well, I think we really have to talk. When can we met up?"

"Green Acres Mall's parking garage, last level, tomorrow midnight, ALONE"

CLICK!

I was more surprise to see Miller still parked outside. I got back into Miller's car.

"SO…"

"I'm going to meet up with him tomorrow night alone."

"You should really think about it before making a decision what if you find something you not ready to deal with?

"I can handle myself out here on these street."

"Don't call me to save you ass."

"Don't worry you'll be my 1st call."

"I'm taking you back home so you can sleep the alcohol it off. I'll talk to you in the morning when you thinking clearly."

FOUR

I fell asleep in the living room waiting for Chuck to return home. I jumped up out of my sleep cause I felt like I was being suffocated by smoke with the taste of fire on my tongue. With my eyes open I realized I was having another nightmare about Brentwood. Wide awake I could still smell the scent of death. I had to make sure Joie was safe. I went into Joie's room to check on her. I almost fainted when I saw Mimi stand at the foot of Joie's bed. Looking at Mimi was like stepping into a time warp. Mimi hadn't aged since her teenage years nor has her style. She had Jordan's on her feet, skin tight jeans, a cropped sweater, with her right shoulder hanging out and them damn two ponytails sitting on the sides of her head. Free use to call Mimi mouse to kid her. Rubbing my eyes didn't change what I was looking at. I thought my eyes were playing tricks on me. But it was really Mimi, in the flesh, standing in Joie's room in my condo. Looking at Mimi I was taken back to the day she gave me Joie. After Brentwood we vowed to stay away from each other. Cutting all tides with each other was the only way we could walk paths away from the tragedy, leaving our dirt behind. But eight months into new beginnings Mimi called me to the hospital. I ran to the hospital to make sure my friend was okay. I didn't know what I was walking into. With Mimi it could range from a black eye to a miscarriage. I had no idea she had given my name as her own. Nor did I had a clue she was even pregnant or had given birth. When I entered her room she was getting dress in a hurry. She asked me to watch her baby while she handle some business with Dom. She couldn't get out of that hospital room fast enough. And she practically ran out the room leaving a trail of smoke. There was no need trying to explain to the nurse that I wasn't the mother cause my name was clearly written on all the documents in Mimi's had writing. The nurse didn't even question my identity cause me and Mimi shared the same face. Now Mimi is just staring down at Joie's seven year old body curled up with her pink bunny "Fluffy" with glassy eyes and wet cheek. Seeing Mimi face filled with emotions reminded me we've come a long way from where we began. I would've never guess that my perfect square life would get so out of shape. Who could predict good vibes shared between me and Mimi would turn into a friendship. A friendship deeper than blood but crystal clear like water. I've always be here for her cause I know she'll do the same for me. The glue between me and Mimi stuck to Free and Tricia, too. And that bond would never be broken. Our love and loyalty will never get lost. When we were teenagers under all circumstances the sister hood come first but now we adults. And as an adult I put my family, Joie and Chuck first. There's an invisible line in our friendship that should never be crossed. And I felt like Mimi running around town, sneaking around with Joie and using my identity was definitely a line crosser. I really wanted to be mad at Mimi but I truly missed her. My eyes look through Mimi and saw the soft side. My mind shuffled through the countless memories we shared. For as long as I can remember Mimi has been in my life. When and where she came from is a secret that died with my mother. For a moment during my childhood I thought I was the only one that could see her until my mother called her by name. The young Mimi didn't talk much. She would play with me in silence. I thought she was a mute until she spoke to me the first day of high school.

"I can't believe you let her draw on the wall?

My yes answer was delivered by a head gestures. I smirked at the question and the memory. Small chuckle escape from under our breath in to the air. When I was the same age as Joie, Mimi had drew on my bedroom walls. I told my mother it was her, even begged my mother to believe me. I will never know if she trusted my word or not cause we were both punished. I insisted that it wasn't me. My mother's explanation for slapping my bottom with five open hand hits and sitting me in the corner on my sore rare end for thirty minutes was for watching Mimi write on the wall and not saying anything. From that point on I told on every bad thing Mimi did and I was still being punished for Mimi's actions, I guess some things will never change. At an early age I learn it was just easier to merge with Mimi. Mimi wipes the sweet loving expression that looked down on Joie out her teary eyes and the monstrous being she truly is revealed. She start to walk toward me and I get a chill from her coldness.

"Chuck is a problem, he has to go." are the words she whispered into my ear as she bumped passed me to exit Joie's room and continued down the plank stairs to the living room. Pushing me is not the greeting I was hoping for after seven years. How dare she? Waltz in here after all this time and start sprouting demands. That was the straw that broke my back. I follow behind her I had a few words she needed to hear.

"How about a damn hello? How about thanking Chuck for taking care of YOUR child like his own for the past five year? I've been nothing but loyal to our friendship. You had a baby in my name. Then I took care of the child like my own. So you could accompany your man on the run from the law who was then caught any way. With Dom in jail I was sure you would come for your daughter but you never showed. Not a birthday or one Christmas. It's been a long way without you, my friend. I was eighteen years old with a new born in my arms. The world rolled their eyes and shook their heads at me. But I walked the long road with my head high and went to college. I earned my business associates degree with many sleepless nights and long wakeful weekends. I wrote papers with wrinkle hurting fingers cause I worked as a dish washer among other side jobs to keep a roof over your daughter's head and food in her stomach. I had to put on my grown woman panties and survive life. Chuck's support help me keep my drive, Joie's unconditional love and sole dependence on me is my motivation. Chuck is my husband and I love him. He is my family now." I had to spit facts at her. She rolls her eyes, sucks her teeth and shifts her body.

"How dare you call him family? The four of us is the only family we have ever known! We are all that we got? Detective Irwin is not you family. Follow me, let me show you what your family has been up too..."

Mimi picks the lock on the door to Chuck's office with a credit card out her back pocket. I wonder what name is on the face of the card. She leads the way into Chuck's office space. I've never entered this room. Its Chuck's personal space it felt weird like I was intruding his mind. I felt uncomfortable between the walls. I stood in the threshold. Mimi walks over to Chuck's desk. She points out two open folders. I followed behind her to the desk to see what she was pointing down at. One folder has everything about Dom's criminal resume. The other folder has pictures of Brentwood's aftermath. I covered my mouth in shock. Chuck what are you looking for?

"His family is the blue shield. How long do you think it's going to take him to figure it out? And when he does piece all the puzzles together what's going to happen to all of us? What happens to Joie? We all going to end in jail, Joie in the system, do you understand what's on the line?"

"I thought I'll never be standing right here, right now talking to you. And you are facing me with all type of information and an ultimatum?"

"Gege, I need you trust me! I'm going what's best for all of us, especially Joie." Mimi's words dripped with sincerity. My heart wanted to believe her but my mind reminded me of her track record, could I ever trust Mimi?

"Listen people are going to come looking for your HUSBAND and this is what you going to tell them. repeat after me... the subpoena from my ex caused us to fight... the fight were small at first and escalated to shouting matches... he had his partner tailing me... we just needed space... no there is nothing going on between me and my ex... he just got out of jail and wanted to see his daughter... I told Dom I was married and all decisions were made with my husband... he didn't like that... that's when I was severed with the subpoena... I honesty wasn't trying to keep him from his daughter... I just had to talk it over with my husband... I never found the right time to tell him..."

I repeated after Mimi verbatim. Tilted my head on certain words to add emotion and battle my eyes in a flirty way on other words. This was how we practice our lies in high school. Mimi not only provide the lie but also adding in the fake body movement to stimulate sensation in the person we were lying too. Mimi is something else. She had concocted this plan weeks ago. At that very moment I know why she told Dom to serve me. It was the back up to the lie. She had me repeat the words over three more times before vanishing as fast as she came. She said somebody will come to ask me about Chuck but until then I'm to live my life as normal. Who's going to ask me about Chuck?

***

Amy has brains that's so smart, it puts my mind at ease. Her touch penetrate pass the skin, her massaging caress emotional sensation. Pure love is so powerful. Love makes me see, smell, taste and touch differently. I can see the beauty in the most ugliest things, thanks to Amy. She has widen my heart and extended my view. We are in the living room on full cuddle mood. I sat in the right corner of the yellow sofa facing the oval bookshelf sectional eyes following the hurricane devastation, Puerto Rico's continuous tragedy and the latest peculiar shooting. My eyes burning from the 60 inch TV broadcasting havoc happening around of the world live from CNN. I'm using the cherry shaped throw pillow as a head rest. Amy's head is laying on my lap. My fingers playing in her hair. The awkward silence could be cut with a knife. Which is unusual for us, after sex we customarily pillow talk, but tonight it's different. The quietness is leaving me to my thoughts. I'm biting my tongue. Mimi has arrived with a vengeance. Her eyes burn for Chuck. Chuck is sniffing around our secret, digging up bones from our pass. Mimi refuse to allow Gege to be separated from Joie due to Chuck blue shield diligence. We could all end up in jail. I needed to talk about it out loud to Amy. In no shape or form do I want Amy involved in whatever is to come with Mimi but I did need to clear my head. I looked down at her sweet face. She has a tear rolling out her left eye over her nose and drops on my pants leg.

"Bae, what's wrong talk to me I here for you." my words and my body moved into sitting position. I wrap my arms around her to bring her closer to comfort. When she's hurting, it hurts me.

"I never told you why I was committed into the juvenile mental institution when I was fourteen years old... I've never met my father. My step-father and mother raised me with all the normal child memories. But when I turned thirteen my step-father started looking at me different. He started sneaking in my room at night with gifts of jewelry, candy or money. I would be excited to hear the creek of my bedroom door's cause I know a gift was coming in. Before I knew it his entrance came with a request, a "gift" from me. The first "gift" was to let him lick on my private area while he pleased himself. And that went on for a few months. His actions made me feel dirty and nasty. I couldn't look myself in the mirror. I try to tell my mother and was slapped in the mouth, so hard she busted my lip open for lying. My mother couldn't comprehended an elite New York lawyer wanted to touch on an adolescent girl when he had a woman with super model body. She just assumed I was retaliating against her decision of not letting me attend a sleepover party. The sleepover was going to be outlet from the touching going on in my bed. The petrified thought of his return would cause me to pee the bed at night. I would just lay in the bed, eyes wide open just waiting to hear that creek in the door. I would psych myself out and end up pissing the bed. He wasn't into urine scent sheets or flesh. Sleeping cold nights in my own urine was my only defense. But the next morning he made it the topic at breakfast. Suggesting something was wrong with me. He threatened if I pee the bed one more night I was going to be sent away. I was baffled that my mother took the time to scold me about wetting the bed but never question how did her husband know about? One night I fell asleep without wetting the bed. When he entered into my bedroom he came with attitude. He slapped my face for talking about the "gift" I gave to him, he push me down for "holding out" on him by wetting the bed. He then roughly inserted two of his fingers inside me while he tugged at his manhood. His fingers was painful but nothing compared to when he ripped my flesh open with his penis. I yelled at the top of my lungs but my mother never come to my rescue. Either she knew and just didn't care or just don't care cause she didn't want to know. But I knew at that point I had to take matters into my own hands. My back was against the wall I had to protect myself! Nobody else would!"

"Tell me, what did you do?"

"I slit his fucking throat. I'm only sorry I didn't fucking kill him! He convinced my mother to commit me into the nut house or he would press charges. I guess my mother was giving me tough love cause in the two years of my stay, not once did she come to visit me. When I was released she still didn't show up. And since then I've been on my own. I'm telling you this cause I'm in love with you and you have been honest about who you are with me. I owe it to you, to let you know who I am and what I'm capable of. And I want to help..."

"Help?"

"Mimi alluded that Joie is under similar distress. And I want you to know I'm here and I want to help... I'm perfect Chuck would never suspect me. I could slit his throat in a blink of an eye."

"Whoa! Slow down! There will be no throat slicing! You can't allow Mimi to contaminate your thinking. She's a master manipulator. She's using your own experience against you."

"I practical raised Joie. The same way I will die for her, I'll kill for her too. I love her like she's my own."

"Hello! Are you even listening to me? Joie is not in any danger! Mimi is a fucking liar! You have too clam down!"

Why would Mimi tell a vicious lie like that? Where's the respect for her own daughter? Mimi's always mingling in somebody's personal life. She is so out of line for even talking to Amy. Amy is mine, not for every one's pleasure. I will not let Mimi ruin this for me. She snatched Erica right from my arms. It took me a very long time to be able to open up again. I watched Amy for weeks before I worked up the nerve just to say hello. When Amy and Gege were in the hospital together, we had a short thing. We were younger, experimenting, no sure of what was really going on. As adults, being with Amy made me realize I've never been truly loved, until now. At this point, I have something that is so valuable and I'll die trying to keep it. Now, I have to spend my precious cuddle time, with the possibilities of a round two, to suck the poison out of Amy's brain. I've visualized me choking life right out of Mimi's evil body. I held Amy silky hands in my hands and looked her in her eyes. I wanted her to not only hear my words but feel them too.

"I love you with all my heart and I couldn't live with myself if something happens to you! I need you to promise me you'll stay away from Mimi, she dangerous!"

***

I entered the "Boy's Lair" with seven eleven slurpies and a bag of assorted junk food, chips, cookies and candy. They were so excited they crowd around me cheering, TRICH! TRICH! TRICH! Like I scored the winning touchdown. I encouraged them to keep cheering. My name being shouted in unisons is my favorite song. I bathe in the adolescent attention showers from Dickey and little friends, Troy and Webster. They were finishing their final auto mechanic project for school, it took them all year to complete. I was only invited cause Dickey wanted to show me off to his friends. I had all three of them hopping around me like it was Easter. I love when people take interest in the one thing I truly love, Me! They were pretending to be all manly. As much as I was fighting back laughter I was enjoying it. I drooled in more way than one as I watch Dickey's lanky body flex and bend. His white tank top t-shirt turn gray covered in grease and oil made him look mature. It was finally time to take a joy ride in the home made car. We all climbed in. The boys are gassed. They were all fueled up off the sugar rush. Within the first three blocks the smell of exhaust filled the inside of the vehicle and we was gasping for air.

"There's a leak in the exhaust system." Webster voice his observance.

"The leak can be in the muffler, exhaust pipe or even the manifold. Shit, we got to find it! Bros, my life depends on this project." Troy needed the pasting grade to graduate. He had the most riding on the project.

Dickey hopped out of the driver's seat and flip the hood of the car open. He wants to show off.

"A car is like a woman. You have to know how to stroke her spots. Calm down boys, the exhaust leaking is coming from the manifold gasket, which is causing exhaust from the combustion chamber to flow the wrong way."

I watch how Dickey move around under the hood of the car and it looked so familiar. He talked though his motions to school the boys. He pointed out the lose gasket. In my teenage years we got around in a beat up Honda Civic. Dom had to pop the top at least once a week. I watch him reboot that shell of a car so many times I even knew a thing a two about under a car hood. Being with Dickey was like jumping back in time. Through Dickey I was getting another chance at my teenage years. I placed my lips on Dickey's lips as a thank you. I didn't anticipate him sticking his tongue in my mouth and wrapping his arm around my back, bringing me close to him. He's being more forward with me. I hoped he was just showing off for his friends. I smiled up at his freckled face and downplayed his actions.

"Can we role play again tonight? I'm hoping for Mimi." his words came with a smack on my butt.

"Mimi?" Oh hell no! I thought it was funny when she pretend to Gege but I always found it to be creepy. Now that she have done it to me I don't know if I should be flattered or to be offended. Ms. Know it all impersonated little oh me. I'm not surprised everybody wants to be like me. They can't so they settle for mimicking my hair, clothes and shoes to best of their ability. But running the sham on Dickey is plain wrong. I kept him at arm length for a reason. Young love tends to get obsessive. I'm wondering, what sexual ride did Mimi take Dickey on, while imagining to be me. It's happening again! She's setting Dickey up just like she did Lippa. But I have a trick for her. I can't even began to explain

Mimi to Dickey's youthful mind. She's a demon that has to be stop or I can save Dickey by leaving him alone.

ABOUT A WEEK AGO...

FIVE

Me and Miller are sitting in a black unmarked 2015 dodge charger. The dodge is our office, cafeteria and home. The awful scent of aged fast food wrappers, empty stale coffee cups and rotten homicide detective smell of decomposed flesh all clogged the air in the dodge. The aroma made my stomach turn flips. My mind tossing around Gege's peculiar behavior lately. The thought of Gege sneaking around had my head aching. My leg just wouldn't stop shaking from the mishmash of everything. My hands are sweating thinking about another man touch my wife. When upset I bit down on my bottom lips. Miller pointed out a blood dot on my lip, apparently I've pierced my lip with my teeth and didn't feel it. Miller has been my partner for two years. We spent twelve out twenty four hours in a day side by side. Miller know more about me than my own mother. We never shared holidays with each other we are family just bind by blue blood. I trusted him with my life and his life is in good hands over here. He knows things about my own wife don't know. He could still see my thoughts as much as I tried to hide them. Yesterday was the first time in the five years of marriage she forgot to pick Joie up from school. That wasn't such a big deal, but for Gege it was big. Gege never forgot anything involving Joie. That little girl is her whole life. But that didn't bother me as much as the humiliation that came with the dispatch calling me into the station to find Joie sitting there. Rule number one as a police officer keep you family and job separate. Immediately I called her cellphone and got the voicemail, twenty eight times in a row. I drove to the flowers shop with sirens blaring just as loud as my anger. I was embarrassed and angry all at the same time. I had earsplitting words for Gege. But when me and Joie arrived we had just missed her according to her assistant Amy. I just took Joie home and waited. She showed up three hours later with a shopping bags and smile on her face. All she had to say for herself was she lost track of time nonchalantly. She casually walked to the room after kissing Joie on the forehead. Gege is perfect patty, everything has a place and she made sure it was in its habitat. But something was off... I've been pacing around in my head trying to figure out the change in my wife. Did I miss something? I'm starting out the Dodge tinted window from the southwest corner on 80th and Third Avenue. We were hoping to catch a person of interest coming to his place of employment to picking up his weekly pay check. But my eyes was looking miles away. My face was red with anger and eyes glassy from the unknown. Miller told me I have nothing to worry about. And to make me rest easy he'll make his brother, Robert, a fellow officer, keep an eye on Gemini. His words were a temporary relief. I decided to clear out the foulness from the car as we wait on our suspect. Miller received a call. The voice on the other end spoke panic into Miller's eyes and distress into his skin color. Just looking at Miller I became spooked. What happened now? At the speed of light Miller jump into the driver's seat, place the siren on the hood of the car and said "Aileen been shot." Aileen is Nathan's little sister. She was taken to Harlem hospital. We zoom up Third Avenue, across the avenues on 125th

street and then straight up Lexon Avenue to 135th street. The speedometer never moved from 100. I'm interested in the back story. Aileen is a little insane after the death of her son. Last year at the precinct Christmas party she attacked Gege referring to her as "Tricia." Miller was completely embarrassed, he was apologizing weeks into the New Year. He had to carry Aileen out of the party cause she kept coming for Gege screaming at that top of her lungs "You killed my son!" At the hospital we flash our badges pass security and walk into the emergency room. Miller forcefully grabs a random doctor by the arm and say "Where's Miller?" Another doctor overheard Miller's terrorizing temper and butted in out of pure fear. The doctor introduced himself and updated Nathan on Aileen's status. It's a flesh wound on her right leg. The bullet went in through her calf hit the bone and exited. No major damaged to the bone, with physical therapy she'll back to 100%. The doctor then led us to Aileen's room. Before Miller could cross the threshold to enter the hospital room, Aileen just started talking...

"Dom shot me!"

"Aileen, just tell me what happened?"

"Dom shot me through the window last night. You know he was released out of jail 3 days ago. I know it was him! Yesterday I saw little James. You remember James?

Miller placed his right hand over his forehead to take in Aileen's gibberish. She wasn't playing with a full deck as is, adding anesthetic to the equation it balance out at straight crazy. First off the surveillance video clearly shows a female shooter. And I know for a fact Dom had been out for two weeks and not three days. I know cause he served Gege with subpoena. But she wasn't home so I was served the court order request for visitation rights of Joie. I had to put my pride to the side and deal with Joie's father but first I have to tell Gege about the subpoena. I've been walking around with the court papers in my pocket for a week already.

"You don't remember James? Little Jimmy?"

Miller's puzzled expression wasn't good enough answer for Aileen. She was going to make Miller's memory picture the kid.

"The damn crayon eating kid!" Aileen shouted with venom.

"Oh yeah, how could I ever forget that kid. I spent two hours with him in the ER, almost missed most of Lippa's third birthday party."

"YES! That him. I saw Little Jimmy and I asked him about that damn girl Tricia. He remembered that Tricia had an elderly aunt Janet that lives on 105ᵗʰ street between second and third avenue. I need you to find the aunt. A.S.A.P! Hopefully the aunt leads us to that little bitch Tricia. And I want Dom arrested NOW!"

"You have to stop this! You're going drive herself crazy! I don't expect you to ever get over the loss of Lippa but you can't continue to live like this. It's unhealthy!"

"I feel it in my heart that bitch had something to do with Lippa's death. Dom paid his debt to society but what about her? She can't get away with no type of punishment! YOU HAVE TO FIND THAT BITCH AND BRING TO JUSTICE! NOOOOOOOOOOOOOOOW!"

Every nurse at the front desk station necks jerked over their shoulder at the instability of Aileen. I gave them a look as if everything was under control but the fact of the matter is Aileen will never be in control again.

"Stop yelling and calm down. Tricia legally didn't commit a crime. So who will punish her?

"So because she didn't physically killed Lippa, she's not responsible? She pulls the strings to make Dom kill his best friend."

"Aileen you have to trust me. I personally know Dom's arresting officer. T.O. (training officer) is by the law. If there was a connection she would've been sitting in jail at the same time as Dom."

"Nathan I need you to believe me. Once that girl became part of their friendship thing started changing. I know my kid and since Dom spent many days and nights at my home for most of his life, I know him just like my own son. They were like brothers with genuine love. The bitch changed them both. And if the law don't have a punishment for that bitch I'll take justice into my own hands!"

"I need you to calm down and don't thinking like that! Me and my partner are going to looking into your shooting and check for more information on the aunt, is that ok boss?

"That great! Please let me know what you find out as soon as you find it!"

I was biting my tongue. For some strange reason I believed Aileen. I had to force my curiosity silence. I have to get all the key dots together before I start drawing lines. Miller felt the need to breakdown the story behind his sister's erratic behavior.

"Eight years ago Aileen's only son, my nephew, Westley Gavin, family calls him Lippa, was beaten to death by Domonique Thomas. My sister feels like it was foul play by "Tricia." Her only proof is the fact that Lippa and Dom grow up together side by side. I read the report, over and over again. I couldn't find anything that ties the girl in. she wasn't even at the scene when Dom was arrested. It's a classic case of, friends turn emeries over a dollar. The police report say Dom beat Lippa over cutting him out of the money deal. The hood version, Dom's girlfriend Tricia is a booster. She would steal beats headphones and Dom would sell the headphones to Lippa making a little profit. Lippa and his girlfriend Nicole Grant then sold the headphone back to their friends. Lippa and Nicole made his money back plus a little extra for their trouble. Then my sister notice Tricia coming by the house without Dom and when Nicole wasn't there. A few weeks later my sister calls me cause a brawl broke out in her apartment. Lippa was caught in the bed with Tricia by Nicole. Tricia and Nicole going at it UFC style. Lippa and my sister trying to keep the girls off each other. A few months go by and Nicole dies in a fire. Then a few weeks later Lippa is beaten to death. My sister is connecting dots that not there. The hood version may or not be true. But the hood version has no cooperative witness, no evidence to support the facts. Case closed. But my sister will not let it rest. She had stalked Dom and his family to the point of them all having orders of protection against her. I don't have the heart to tell her I can't go nowhere near a closed case with a conviction and an order of protection on the Miller name."

I haven't opened up to Miller about my curse case. At that moment I was so glad that I've never told him anything without any proof. He would be treating me like I was Aileen. But I have a feeling Aileen is on to something. Could her Tricia and my Tricia be the same person? There's a connection between my curse case, Lippa's death and Tricia. But how will I get the proof? It has to be undeniable facts to get Miller on board to close these cases. We drove over to PSA5 on 115th street and Madison Avenue. We are meeting up with the officers investigating the shooting at Aileen's apartment. All four of us greeted each other with respect. We all stood over the technician replaying the surveillance camera planted inside a street light post outside of Aileen's window. My mouth dropped open from the image on the screen. I used my right hand to cover my mouth I didn't want my disbelief to escape. I can't believe my eyes. If I didn't know any better I would swear the woman is shaped just like Gege. The technician paused and printed the image. It was a woman dressed in all black, black ski mask and a red leather motorcycle jacket. Everything in my heart want to go back to the hospital and show Aileen the print-out but I didn't want to play with her sanity. I took my own copy of the image from the surveillance camera and headed to the station I needed Dom's file. I reached the police station in Riverdale in record time after I drop Miller's off at the hospital. Aileen hasn't stop calling him since we left the hospital. I immediately dug up Dom's case file on the computer screen, secretly printing each page. My eyes went through each word like a fine tooth comb. By reading his file I learned he is petty low level criminal. Gege what was going with this street trash? I can't image his filthy hands touching my decent wife. I ran "Domonique Thomas" name through United States data base. I was floored to discover Joie Thomas's birth certificate born to Gemini Patricia Freeman and Domonique Thomas. My eyes refuse to fight back the tears of pain. Why would she lie to me? I didn't care that she came with a plus one. I even offered to adopt Joie to make our family complete but Gege insisted that she wasn't the mother, making that kind of decision was out of her hands. But here it is in black and white, she is Joie's mother and Domonique Thomas is Joie's father. Finding this Tricia is more urgent than ever, now. The new information had my brain in over load. I need a drink. I entered a random bar with only one objective, to get drunk. I sat down on a stool right in the middle of the bar. I couldn't help myself, I'm a cop by nature. By taking this seat I have an eagle-eye from the front door to the emergency exit in the back. Behind the charming bartender, Kelly, is about a hundred bottles of various liquor on the mirror wall. Through the mirror my observant eyes could see behind me. There's a total of eleven people in the bar, including the Kelly, the bartender and myself. It was so comical that I had to chuckle at myself.

"What's so funny?" Kelly's question came after she planted her elbows on the bar top, her hand cupped her jawline creating a direct eye shot of her C cup breast.

"I'm just laughing at myself, I'm such a cop. I can't turn it off."

"Something like a spidey sense?"

"Funny, but yes. Watch I can show you..."
"Besides you and I there are nine other people here. My sharp eyes first notice the middle age gentleman at the right end of the bar, sipping on his second glass of scotch, straight no ice. He's wearing a blue and red plaid long sleeve button up, tan slacks and shiny burgundy penny loaves, no socks, with a worn down heels. His eyes engage with 85 inch TV mounted over the glass mirror wall behind the bar. The TV is providing the HD experience to the Giants verses the Cowboys match up. He's a family man, with a child younger than a year old. I can tell from the dried up baby formula on the left side of his collar. He had to resort to the bar to watch the game in peace without game's sound being over shadow by his wife's and children's voices. My third eye took special attention to a woman sitting at

the left end of the bar. She has dark shoulder length hair, mascara running down her cheeks and red lipstick is smeared outside her lip line. Perhaps, her black dress means she's mourning a death. That would explain the misplacement of her womanly face paint. She's accompanied by another woman also dressed in black. One minute they were laughing next minute they were crying. Clearly they were drinking over memories. Behind me are the third, fourth and fifth persons sitting at one of the three tables under the dim light are all guys. Game watchers all wearing Cowboy t-shirts. Screaming and yelling for every play in the favor of the Cowboys. Of course the adult frat boys are chugalugging beer and chips. To the right of the frat adults is a blonde headed female, with a mole on right cheekbone, babysitting a half full beer mug. Sitting next to blondie is a bald head, green eye gentleman on his second beer mug. The newly couple are also game watchers with their matching Giant t-shirts. It was only two of them but they roared like a crowd at the frat boys when the Giant made a play closer to a touchdown. The eighth and ninth persons in the bar are at the pool table across from the back end of the bar. There were two gentleman, one young male, one older male. The younger one has on light gray sweat pants, white sneakers and white shirt with a red writing that reads "Above the rim". The older one dressing like his age. His plain worn jeans and actual cowboy jersey number twenty-one, Elliott, and dirty sneakers. They share similar facial features. They are definitely related. I'm certain I heard the older male call the younger male "son" more than once. It conceivably that they are bonding over the pool game, adding beer to liberate the tongue." I opened my eyes and looked around just to confirm my blind observation.

"WOW! I'm impressed, you should audition for the show "Super Human" that was amazing, next drink on me Mr. Officer."

See, I was born into the blue. My father was a cop and his father also living under the blue shield. My father would always shout "It's in the blood." For as long as I could remember he was grooming me for the job. Every good law enforcer should have "eyes like a hawk" and a set of "dog ears." Any and every time we enter any restaurant, family gathering, or just at the super market I was quizzed about random people, places and things descriptions. I'm a natural. My hawk eye earned me a hall monitor sash. I wore that sash like my father wore his badge, with honor and respect. My classmate didn't appreciate my commitment to the sash. I quickly picked up boxing skills, from my cousin to protect my square lifestyle. My cousin lived on the next block over in the same extract spot as my house is. Our backyards connected. So I grew up in two houses. My cousin and I, are our parent's only children. We are born a month apart. We did everything together just like siblings. Shannon is the brother I wished for, only thing she's a girl. Not just any girl. She could take a hit in football, hand skills like a boxer, and she has enough class to also be a lady. Shannon moved to LA after her eighteenth birthday. She preferred a camera's flashing lights over flaring sirens. We talk every night. She's not only family she's my best friend. My Uncle Steven and Aunt Holli still lives in the same house and my mother still stay in the house I grew up in. After my father died in the line of duty my mother rarely comes out but Holli keeps a good eye on her. I sat at the bar being baited into conversation by Kelly as she continued a flow of drinks on my tab. I entertained her to keep my mind from falling apart from the bits and pieces of facts I have gathered. In came a saucy sexy woman with two ponytails sitting on the sides of her head. Turning my head wasn't giving me a good view, I turned my whole body to face the door to get a better look at the beautiful creature creeping in. She lock eyes with me from the time she entered the bar. She walk straight forward right into my eyes. I stop counting how many drinks I had after the fourth double shot of "Irish water" in my father's words, which is Jameson whiskey. So I can say with confidence I am drunk. The sexy woman took a sit right next to me. My body stiffen in more ways than one. I couldn't turn back around cause I couldn't stop starring. I've gazed into her eyes before and that wasn't the liquor talking. I've tasted those lips. Her shirt danced off her skin leaving her left shoulder exposed and her black mini shirt showed off her suggestive legs. My lips watered for another taste of the familiar skin. I took a deep breathe trying to regain consciousness but instead her familiar sweet scent danced into my nose. I rub my eyes to clear my sight. It felt like I had blinked and we were at a hotel. The alcohol started playing tricks on my vision. The sexy woman from the bar, familiar facial features turned into my wife's characteristics, even the skin qualities was the same. But no matter the lies my eyes tell, I knew it wasn't my wife this women is doing things my wife will never do. She led me by the hand to the hotel room. She pulled my hand like she was handling a dog leach. I followed like a lost puppy panting after her tail. Once we were in the room. She push me up against the wall and shoved her tongue in my mouth. She had slide her hand down my pants. Her soft touch stroking my skin closed my eyes as I begged for more. I got sucked into it and wrapped my arms around her back to pull her body close to me. She pulled away from the kiss, dragging my bottom lip through her teeth. The tingling sensation of pain travel from my lips and I push her body down onto the rented white sheets. I'm fully excited by the woman's fight back.

My wife is passive to my aggression during sex. The woman with my wife's face is feisty. With proper protection I dove into familiar water. She stop me by planting her feet on my chest. The more I leaned followed the harder she pushed back. I grabbed both of her ankles and spread her legs wide open. By pulling her legs apart the motion pulled her skirt up to her waist. I ripped her panties off with my teeth. I enjoy drinking the free flowing water from her lips. I returned the favor of lightly biting her lips. She even moans like my wife. Forcefully I filling her inside with latex coated pleasure while felling into her eyes. She pull me in deeper by hugging my body. My strokes overflowed with anger for my wife. By force of habit I started voicing my rage with my wrath. Her nail scrap my back, pulling up flesh. The slashes to my back made me throw harder swings. Her yells of pain and pleasure ring in my ear. Next thing I remember is waking up at six am in a hotel bed alone with a screaming headache and shrieking scratches on my back. My head is swimming in a thousand intoxicating questions. My mind couldn't separate the woman's face from my wife's face. Did the woman even exist? My head was pounding beating at the facts colliding together in my mind. I hop into my car my thoughts are driving me crazy. My mind wheel over the information I already have. Domonique Thomas's tattoo tells he have permanently joined to Gege, Mimi, Tricia and Free. The link between him and my wife is Joie's birth certificate. Aileen is the proof of he's connected to Tricia. Tricia is directly tied into the burnt teenagers. If I can get Veronika Patterson, the mother of Erica Patterson, one of the burnt teenagers to identify Aileen's shooter as "Tricia" I'll be a step in the right direction. I've already ran the name "Janet" with the 105th street, New York, NY 10029 address in the new Social Security benefits date base. The system give back 3 names matching the filters. I couldn't even speak my wife's name cause I'm so annoyed by her secrecy. Looking at her is out of the question until I have some of my own answers. I pull up to garage door in front of my mother's house. I couldn't explain spending the night out nor did I have a justification for the tingling scratches on my back. The best thing to do was get freshened up at my mother's before going to work.

"Morning mother." As I entered I greeted my mother with words, a kiss and a hug. I took a seat at the kitchen table. My mouth watered for the fresh smell of cooked home fries and scrambled eggs.

"Trouble in paradise? You look like you slept under a rock." She spoke as she sat a plate in front of me with a nice cup of coffee.

It was like déjà vu. Breakfast at the Irvin's is the time my mother prey on information.

"No today Mom."

"Ever since you were a little boy you would bring home wound birds, sick dogs and homeless cats. I see some things never change."

"Mother please don't refer to my wife as a hurt animal." I had to excuse myself from the table. I shoved three spoonful of the home fries and eggs. I grab my toast with my mouth and my right had snatched up the cup of coffee. I foresee my mother's words ahead.

"They say charity begins at home. What about me? No grandchildren in five years, what's the hold up? I want to have the sweet sound of children running around. The tender noise of yelling and crying! I'm going to die with no grandchildren, is that what you want?"

"Joie is available anytime!"

"That is not my grandchild!"

I had to walk away from my mother to stop the insults. My mother didn't have a reason why she rejected my wife and step child she just wouldn't accepted them. She made it her business to make them uncomfortable by bring her pet, Ashley around. I didn't have the energy to fight a losing war. My mother is always right when she's wrong. I entered my old bedroom upstairs. Everything right where I left it years ago. My elementary school hall monitor sash hanging of the bed headboard. Drooping of the closet door knob is my red court room tie from middle school. I remember when I came home with the news. My father was more excited than me. Student council is kid's courts over seen by Mr. Lawson. Mr. Lawson was a retired lawyer who taught at my school. The council was faced with disciplinary cases. I had memorized the school policy reference book and the student rule booklet. I could quote guidelines from either handbook in my sleep. As student body council we weighted facts and remorse, then decided the student's fate. This position came with money, power and respect. Middle school students would pay to sway my vote, my integrity wouldn't allow me to ever take a bribe. My power was in the respect given when I walked the halls. Court was held twice a month and twice a month I would wear my navy blue church suite, white button up shirt and my infamous red tie. As I touch the tie I can see the glow in my father's eyes, the spark made me feel like a king. On top of my dresser is the trophy I received when I won the baseball championship at the academy. The coach said my curve ball is major league worthy but my father couldn't hear anything other than code blue. He actually cried when I graduated from Junior Police Academy, a summer program. Let me be the first to tell this academy wasn't no walk in the park. The physical training pushed the mind body and spirit. What was left of my mind was booked with a crash course introduction to criminal law. The "fun" part were the CPR/First Aide class, evidence collection, and fingerprinting but nothing beats riding with a real cop on duty during a mock traffic stop. The speed radar was the coolest thing my juvenile eyes ever seen. Next to the academy trophy is a store bought speed radar my father bought me for my fourteenth birthday. The academy's "hands-on" environment and certificate made me believe I was on the force already. By high school I drooled for the blue blood. For four summers I worked summer youth at the academy. The staff uniform resemble the state issued uniform. I knew it was just fabric but it felt like I was superman putting on his cape. Straight out of high school my father enrolled me into the Cadet Corps. I think he had my spot reserved since I was born. Ever been somewhere for the first time but everybody knows your name? That what entering the cadets felt like. The cadets was enough on my plate but I had a nice desert of a full-time college student schedule. Hanging in the closet, right behind my academy staff uniform is my cadet uniform and in front of it all was my academy student uniform. Finally after three years of hard work, at last I'm official police officer. It also happened to be the same year my father was killed and when I meet my wife. I felt like my father sent Gege my way. She came into my life when I really needed to be loved. I stood in the center of the bedroom and looked around like flipping through images of my childhood. I'm proud of my youthful certificates, plaques, trophy they are my payments of homage to my father. It's a privilege to represent the blue. There was a time when a police officer was a hero to the community. I still live in that time. My father taught me "let a man actions represent his character. The system is lopsided, it's our job to balance it out. Some of this kids don't have a fighting chance but you can be the one to give them that one win. And the feeling of a win can empower them to keep winning." My father has sponsored sneakers, education and housing to youth that was once in trouble with the law now living by the law. My father was a powerful man. He start a center in the heart of El Barrio, Spanish Harlem, giving teenagers a place to just hang out safely. He gave them little odd job in which he paid them out his own pocket. I am his only son but he has fathered plenty. I had to shower and wash away the feeling of missing my father and get ready to go work, and my make my father smile from heaven. As the warm soapy water cascade own my body I almost jumped out of my skin from the water burning the gashes on my back. Blinded by water I reached for a towel. I rub the towel over my face. With the regain of sight I couldn't believe my eyes.

"Wow! I would've never guess Gemini was the "I like it rough" type. I can make you feel better."

The words flew out of Ashley's mouth as her hand took the air and reached for my junk. I swatted the back of her right hand. In spite of her being my mother number one draft pick for me since middle high school, I wasn't interested then and certainty not now. Ashley Collon is Shannon's childhood friend. Ashley lived three blocks over but could never find her way home. Ashley is like the furniture in the living room that's been there for years and you only notice it when you trip over it. It was one drunk night a long long time ago, in college, it meant nothing and to be honest I really don't remember it. But she held the night like a dog with a bone. She dropped to her knees on the bathroom floor. Her puppy dog eyes begs to please. I wrapped the towel around my waist and brushed by her. She try to pull at my towel as I pass her. I grab her right waist pulled her up to her feet, looked deep into her eyes and spoke right to her heart...

"Ashley, this is never going to happen! You are disrespecting my marriage by even being in this bathroom right now! By touching and grabbing on me you're disrespecting me! And dropping to your knees for a married man, is disrespecting yourself! I think you should excuse yourself before you find out how rough my wife can really get."

Three weeks ago...

SIX

Some people spend their whole life without ever experiencing true love. I've been lucky enough to find true love with my soul mate. I'll be loving this man until my last breathe with love as fresh at the first day I met him at the tender age of thirteen. He was five years older than me but age don't matter to soul mates. He understand me without me explaining. It's amazing how people fell in love. I remember the day I met Dom like it was yesterday. Gege was a walking target for bullies and jokes. She's kind hearted, soft spoken and afraid of saying no. Her mother was sick and suffering. Before her mother died in the fire she was already dead inside. When Gege's father looked at Gege, he saw the future he had planned out with his wife. As Gege's mother's presences fade so did Gege in her father's sight. Before long she was completely invisible to her father. She was walking through her days. Combing her hair, showering and wearing clean clothes was optional for Gege. I didn't think Gege should've be dealing with a bunch of mean spirited girls with foul mouths, she was going through enough. So I did what I've always done, look out for her. I defend Gege against the group of mean girls. They laughed at me like I was a joke. So I showed them a trick. As I knocked teeth out their mouth with my master combination lock hanging on a shoe string. Dom grab me from behind, wrapping his strong long arms around my body and whispered in my ear "Shawty, you wilding! Popo coming for sure, you got to get out of here, NOW!" Then he let me go. I turned around and looked up into his pretty light brown eyes and saw a spark. My mind know he was right but it felt like my shoes were filled with cement. I couldn't move. Dom's right hand grab my left hand and lead me away from harm's way. I wanted to know everything about him and he answered every question I had. He grow up in a single mother home in Patterson Projects in the Bronx. He has a half-brother from his father but he don't know him like that. He has a friend slash brother he grow up with that he considered blood. He had done some things he not proud of but they were necessary. "There's not rules to feeding your family." Sixty days before we met he was release from juvenile detention center on his eighteenth birthday. It was destiny for us to be at the same place at the same time. We both known something long-term was starting. When we kissed it was like a thousand star shine over us. When he wraps my body in his arm and my head is resting on his chest I can hear our hearts beat in unisons. Gege's mother had a problem with Dom from day one. I know I'm not suppose to speak ill of the dead but who I date was none of her business GeGe is her daughter not me. She made Dom a daily discussion. I just couldn't take the rhetoric. It was nice that she was looking out for her daughter's friend but at some point enough is enough. Not a person, place or thing could keep me from Dom. I'm sorry she gone for Gege but she wouldn't be miss by me. From the day we met to every day forward for the next five years we were an inseparable team. He was arrested and severed seven years for beating Lippa to death. Loyalty should be in the bloodstream of brothers. Lippa crossed Dom in two ways. Lippa was feeding Nicole information about Dom's business which was none of her business. Dom didn't care if Lippa know or not that Nicole was working with police. Lippa's pillow talking was against the bro code and was building a case against Dom. Then Lippa convinced Tricia to cut Dom out of the headphone hustle. Then to add salt to an open wound Lippa robbed Tricia. Lippa had the nerve to try to blackmail Dom. Lippa thought he was untouchable in the street because his uncle was a rookie police officer. But Dom told Lippa more than once if you going to play in the street you play by street rules can't call in the law when shit don't go his way. Aileen, Lippa's mother is a die hard. Dom going to jail and serving his time wasn't good enough she needed to know every detail. But who want to tell somebody's mother their son was a slime ball. Dom couldn't bring himself to say the ugly words so he avoided her with an order of protection. My leg is shaking with anticipation. Dom was locked up and so was I. Once I have experience real love it's hard to live without it and to not live for seven years is more was living in hell. And seven years of burning on the inside is a very long time, it was pure torture. Today makes twelve years since I met Dom and I fall deeper in love with him, every day falling even further in love. I'm standing outside the prison gate waiting for Dom with loving arms. After Dom beat Lippa to death we was on the run for three months. Dom wouldn't allow himself to miss the birth of Joie. So we was riding around the city in Ms. Janet's run downed '97 Honda Civic during the day and sleeping at various hotels at night. We drove up and down the coast. Sometime we stood in hotels in Philadelphia and in Connecticut. Occasionally, we even stood in the city with all the risk. I can't image how I did it with that big belly full of baby, it had to be the power of love. It wasn't a planned pregnancy but she was more than welcome. Me and Dom put all our energy into our baby growing inside of me. Although we were on the road ninety five percent of the time I ate nutritional food. We were more than excited watching her grow and move around from the outside. Dom being the supportive father every step of the way. Playing house while in love was like living in a bubble. Brentwood felt like years in the past when it as only a few months. Being pregnant was the perfect distraction from the events that took place in Brentwood. Spending every waking second with Dom was the perfect diversion from missing my friends. Pregnancy came with emotional instability. I wanted Gege to mother me. I needed Free to rant about the nontoxic verses toxic baby product. I could've used some of Tricia vanity tips to keep my sexy while my feet and hand swell. But I had set the rule of not contacting each other I would look foolish to be the first one to reach out, so I didn't. After I gave birth to Joie which means joy in French, I had to put my pride to the side and call Gege. Dom was still on the run we couldn't just sit in the hospital and wait for police to arrest him. We couldn't take the baby on the run with us. Gege was the best choice beside the fact I used her state ID and her health insurance card for admissions. Dom agreed to GeGe holding down Joie. I was face with an important decision I had to pick between my newborn baby and Dom. I refused to live without Dom, it was impossible. When we left the hospital leaving Joie in Gege arms, I saw a few drops fall from Dom's eyes. I know it sounds selfish but is didn't want to share

Dom's love with Joie. The next morning out of the blue he woke up and said he didn't want to run no more. He want us to all live together as a family. And to do that he had to turn himself in. I cried like a baby I couldn't imagine living without Dom. We spent the last forty eight hours in a hotel just talking and holding each other. Dom understood every part of me and for that I will forever love him. I know now it was Dom's way of trying to prepare me for the next seven years without him but nothing could compose me for that. I woke up in a hotel bed alone. I ran to the hotel bathroom and turn the shower on with the water streaming hot. I was waiting for the stream to reveal Dom's message written on the mirror. "I love you, I want us all to be free! I'll be back for all of yous!" The words were just like a knife going through my chest, my heart was hurt. I curled into a ball and stop living. There was no life without Dom. knowing Dom's release date was approaching it was as if I was getting another chance at love. As the time wind down my heart started pulsating and I could feel him getting closer. I could spot him in a million man march. He's being escorted to the gate by a correctional officer. Every step he took closer, my heart beat harder. As soon as his body was outside the gate I ran into his arms. He lift me up with a hug. Oh his arm felt like home. I wrapped my arms around his neck and tied my legs around his waist. Planting a thousand kisses all on his face. I missed Dom with all my heart. Dom knew all parts of me and still loved me. Being in Dom's arms made me feel alive, truly living. I could feel his skin but it still didn't feel real. It's a dream come true. I want to taste him. I was pulling on his zipper while my tongue surf in his mouth. He could've took me right there on the spot in front of Riker's islands gates. Our seven years of lust is over flowing we couldn't make it to the hotel. We climb into the back seat of the Gege's car. Yes I borrowed her car. What she don't know won't hurt her. I didn't know how thirsty I was until I tasted his flesh. My lips and tongue bouncing up and down on his shaft. He sung praises of pleasure. His voice was like a 90's R&B song. When the melody make your heart soft and the words make you feel warm inside. The pleasure and pressure squeezed seeds from his loins. His leg was still shaking after the fact. Dom was eager to be behind the wheel he hadn't driven in seven years. As fast as he drove we still couldn't get to the hotel fast enough. I didn't want go to some rinky dink hotel on Dom's first day home. I had money to splurge. Of course Dom wanted in on the new hustle. Just like with the black boxes, I like doing wire transfers, easy and untraceable. The new hustle is bitcoins, Europe money. I freeze corporation's servers and hold them for twenty thousand bitcoin ransom. The bitcoins are transferred to an overseas account. Overseas the bitcoins are converted into US dollars by a shady foreign exchange company. The conversion is, for every bitcoin it's equivalent to one dollar and forty nine cent in US money. Dom loves to hear the details of my hustles. He wanted to know how I access the computer servers. Gege's flower shop deliveries to corporate offices is my admission. Dom couldn't hold back his laughter. He know Gege had no idea her shop was being used for my hustle. She would have a tantrum. Since Gege came up in conversation I had to exposed her for marry Chuck. I wanted her to keep an eye on Chuck not fall in love and marry him. Chuck was going to become a problem. I told Dom to file for visitation right of Joie. By Dom filing the paper work Chuck will come to him. We still had Aileen's crazy ass to deal with. And if the situation wasn't already bad it gets worst. Chuck's partner is Aileen's brother. But that's talk is for later. Right now I needed to show Dom just how much I missed him by exploring every inch of his body with my lips, tongue and hands. But first I had to bathe that nasty smell of jail off my man. The luxurious hotel in downtown Brooklyn took Dom's breathe away. He was taken aback by the view of the Brooklyn Bridge and the coast of Manhattan in the background. As soon as the sky turned off and lights sparkled under the dark sky. By day the bridge and coast was unnoticeable but at night it came alive. Dom stood behind me. Looking at the light with Dom's right arm over my shoulder across my chest and his penis pressed up again my bottom igniting a warm feeling through my insides. It was a sight I wouldn't want to share with nobody else. Dom is handcrafted just for me. A candle lit lobster dinner under the stars in towel robes being served like a King and Queen on the balcony had Dom smiling from ear to ear. We toast our champagne glasses to new beginnings. After dinner I was Dom's desert. Under the city lights it was a race who could get out of their robe quicker. We wanted each other so bad we would've ripped through each other's skin just to get to one another. We push and pull each other's bodies like magnets do. I could tell he was thinking about my touch the whole time he was gone. He was dripping sweat, eating cake and sucking on toes. He went three rounds with ease, from the chair to the bed spilling onto the floor. I was completely wiped out. Dom wanted to see Joie. I had to talk him down. We had to follow the plan or we won't never see Joie. I turned on the TV as we cuddle in the bed.

News reporter, "Police released this footage of the shooter. The person in the red leather jacket shot into an apartment window near Patterson public housing. The bullets went through the window and went through the victim's leg. Police department is releasing this image of the shooter. Any information in helpful. Please contact 1-800-577-tips."
I'm going to set Tricia's fucking jacket on fire, I swear, if it's the last thing I do. I

wish I could just lay here bathing in Dom's presence and just watch him sleep but I had to do what I all have do. Clean up after Gege and Tricia. I kissed Dom's sleeping face. I really didn't want to go but I had to...

PRESENT

I'm in a half-conscious state but my body is absence of external response. Why am I standing in the condo's parking garage? I'm watching Dickey messing around with Chuck's car, the hood is propped open. I'm yelling at him to stop! My shouts are asking him what's he doing? Why he can't hear me? Dickey hears Chuck walking toward him. Dickey ducks into the shadows of walls. I'm yelling at Chuck not to get into the car. Am I a ghost? Have I died? I'm waving my arms trying to flag down Chuck's attention. I don't know what Dickey did to Chuck's car but I know it wasn't good. My stomach ached with fear. In my face Chuck drove off. My heart was pounding I wanted to stand in front of his car but I'm invisible. Chuck pull into Green Acres Mall's parking garage. Why am I here? Chuck could barely keep his eyes open. He was practically falling asleep behind the wheel. He opens the driver's side window to get some air. I could smell the carbon monoxide pouring out from the inside of the car. Chuck is dizzy and light head from inhaling the toxic gas. I saw Amy and Mimi hiding behind a parked car. I felt like I was watching a horror movie and I wanted to warn the unsuspecting victim, danger is ahead. I cry and yell for Chuck to just drive off. But he wasn't listening to me. I started kicking a garbage can. Hoping the commotion would get him to look my way. He didn't look my way. I'm hollering at him, not to get out of the car. Amy crawls around the exterior of car, she slither into the back seat of Chuck's car. Oh my goodness, she has a knife. Amy has a weird look in her eyes. It was definitely Amy but she wasn't herself at all. She titled his groggy forehead back with her glove covered left hand and with a swift swing of her right hand she ran the knife across his neck. The blade on his skin sounded like a little whistle of death. The knife split his skin open smooth like it was butter. Chuck's blood squirted out on to window shield and dash board, like a bitten open ketchup packet. I wanted my vision to be a hallucination. I was helpless I couldn't save Chuck. I bite my arm to wake up from this horrible nightmare. I want to know how and when did Amy meet Mimi?

Amy gets out the car and assist Mimi. Together they pour gasoline on the Chuck's lifeless body, the passenger's seat, the back seat and on the outside of the car. Mimi lights a match and throws it on Chuck's lap and slammed the car door shut. The mix of carbon monoxide, gasoline and fire created a combustion of flames two feet high and heat over a thousand degrees. Nothing could survive that kind of heat...

I jumped up! I quickly look around in a panic. To my relief I'm in my condo's living room. I ran upstairs to see if Chuck came home. My bed was unslept in. I immediately starting dialing his cell phone number. It had to be a dream. But when I checked my arm the bite was there. I went to the kitchen to get a cup of coffee to get my thoughts together. My chest ached. It felt like I'm not going to see Chuck again. I turn on the TV.

"Good Saturday morning, New York. I'm Ashley Collon and its 6 am, record high for toady is 70 degrees outside with lots of sun. Breaking news, Long Island police department is asking the public for help. This morning a burning body was found in Green Acres Mall's parking garage. The singed remains are unidentifiable. Long Island police department is pleading with the community if anyone see anything or knows anything contact 1-800-577-TIPS."

The last thing I need was hearing Ashley's holier than thou voice. In the five years of marriage it was one other time that Chuck has spent the night out and returned with scratches. That happened about three weeks ago. I wonder is he the one really having an affair and trying to flip this on me? I stood up most of the night pacing the floor worried about Chuck mixed with anger. One minute I was crying to the heavens praying he was okay. Then the next second I was cussing his name hoping he was alive so I could kill him. The emotional roller coaster of a police officer's wife is similar to the wife of a hustler. I spent many nights up with Mimi worried if Dom would return from working the streets. The streets are unpredictable for both sides. As I was showering and getting dress Lyla, Lynn's sixteen year old daughter ranged the doorbell. She is Joie's babysitter for the next six hours. Today is the biggest contract my flower shop has acquired since the doors been open. I had to keep telling myself it's all a dream. Chuck is somewhere skulking over Dom. The Dom issue is something I plan of fixing very soon. I needed my mind focus on today's wedding of Riverdale's councilman, Matthew Amboy's daughter, Katherine. The wedding is being held at Riverdale's largest church. Twenty pews on each side of the church. It's common to decorate the pews down the aisle to the church's alter. But Katherine is definitely not common. Bridezilla has nothing on Katherine. She need floral arrangements on both sides of the pews, totaling eighty arrangements. She needs a floral arch over the church's alter, for the pictures, of course. The flower girl would be sprinkling the bride's runway with white rose petals. Then there was the bride's and bridesmaid's bouquets. Also the groom and groomsman corsages were on the list. Katherine wanted everyone who drove by the church to know a wedding was in progress so the entry step banisters had to be draped with floral arrangement. Oh did I mention she need fresh flowers. Fresh flowers are beautiful but they are very finicky. The wrong temperature or the lightening in the church could cause the flowers to wither quickly. I arrived to shop at seven thirty and Amy, the assistant of the year, was already at the shop working. I was biting my lip. I was fighting the urge to ask her where was she last night? Amy had all eighty arrangement boxed in the refrigerator ready to go. We was pushing against the clock. We couldn't get into the church until nine and the wedding begins at noon. We had three hours to mount the arrangements. The only good thing is the church is walking distance from the shop. With the window of idle time we made final touches on the floral arrangements that will be placed at the eighty table wedding reception starting at four pm. So once the church is set up we had to drive one hour and a half to Dover Plains, New York to the Amboy's family mansion. The whole drive Amy's heart was bleeding for the poor body that was burnt to death in the Green Acres Mall. She prayed for the family. "It had to be the most nerve racking thing ever to just not know what happened to a loved one." Is she testing me to see if I know it was her? Or that it's Chuck's burnt body? I played dumb and didn't entertain her conversation. The drive is sixty nine miles long. I was on my feet from seven thirty am to three pm. I was exhausted. But resting wasn't an option in one hour Dom was going to have his first supervised visit with Joie. Yes the family court judge said "This court is all about family. The state of New York will not stand in the way of a father and his child. I'm granting Domonique Thomas supervised visitation every other Saturday from 4pm to 7pm." My lawyer explained "supervised visitation" meant that I would have to I drop Joie off at a center. I would be asked to leave and return when visiting hours were over. I was totally confused about the supervised part. The visit is supervised by a court appointee. I had all type of mixed emotions and I haven't even talk to Joie about it yet. I was hoping my lawyer would've stop the court order before the day came. Well the day is today. But I wasn't to fatigue to stop by the Riverdale police station on my way back from Dover Plains. I was hoping to talk to Chuck about where has he been and I needed some spousal support with the Dom visitation situation. On the front steps of the police department I ran into Ms. Ashley. My mind started envisioning

Chuck and Ashley having wild sex. Sex so wild he ended up with scratches on his back. But before I could say a word Ashley started talking.

"I'm here on strictly business..." she answered the look on my face. "I'm working the burning body story. I came here to see if Chuck could give me an exclusive, but he's not here and his partner don't know where he is either. Do you know where he could be?"

No I don't know where my husband is. And if I did Ashley would be the last person I would tell. I'm worried about Chuck. He would never miss a day of work. He loves being a cop. I'm more concerned than mad at Chuck but now I'm completely in panic mood. I know Chuck wasn't in the precinct but I wanted to see if I could squeeze some info from his partner Nathan. Nathan's eyes were red and puffy like he's agonizing over something. Before I could ask him anything he started questing me. "When was the last time I saw Chuck? "Did I know who Chuck went to meet last night?" he's questions are being shot faster than a semi-automatic. Did something happen to Chuck? He was unclear. Chuck was working a case last night and haven't been located yet. I heard Nathan's words but he was hiding something. Was the dream real? The tears started flowing and I couldn't stop it. I need Chuck to be okay. I had to pull myself together for Joie. I'm on my way to her. I pick Joie up from Saturday cooking class. She wouldn't let me get a word in. She was over excited about her sweet potato and Yukon potato puree blend. I was also distracted by the savoy butter sweet taste, nothing short of amazing. So good I went back for seconds. But I had to give Joie the prep talk about meeting Dom for the first time. But she prepped me.

"I know I'm going to see my father today. I also know he can't take care of me because he's a criminal. You don't have to worry he'll never hurt me. He just wants see me again cause I have his eyes."

"Who told you that?"

"Ms. Mimi, she really nice."

"When did you talk to Mimi?"

"Sometimes she bring snacks to me at school. You two could be twins. She looks like you playing dress up."

I was speechless. Mimi has gone too far yet again. No, I didn't have any problem with Mimi talking to her daughter but I should at least be notify. Joie is very mature for a seven year old. Her understanding level is above a common teenager. But since I'm raising her I should be in charge of what she is exposed to, right? I wondered how did Mimi introduce herself to Joie? Joie is very smart I'm sure she questioned Mimi about her identity. I sneaked the question in on Joie. I don't know Mimi's plan but deceiving Joie and introduce herself as an "Aunt" just don't set well with me. What if in the future it's revealed that Mimi is actually Joie's mother? Information like that is enough to destroy a child's mental state. Now that I will not stand for. Joie is my reason for living. Her smile is my sunshine at any time of the day. Her laughter so pure it slips into me and tickle my heart. With my heart pounding I handed my most precious part of my life over to Mrs. Carla Nelson, court appointee of supervised visitation. Once in my car I call Mimi. I dialed the number she had given to Joie for emergencies. I didn't know what I was going to say but I needed to know the logic behind her movements. I planned on slowly preparing Joie for this day but kept putting it off. I just couldn't find the right words to say. Just when I thought my day couldn't get any worst, I get a phone call from Free. Free has been arrested for protesting at Trump's tower and she needs me to come pick her up from central bookings. The whole criminal act caught on the five o'clock news. The publicity had her go through the system in record time. She was arrested at four pm and being released at six pm. I had one hour to pick up and drop off Free and be back by seven to pick up Joie. I had plenty of time since I had to drop Joie off at a family center near Brough Hall, downtown Brooklyn. From the family center to centra bookings is a straight shot. From the time they signed Free over to me to this very moment she hasn't stop talking.

"I just can't believe the American people put a raciest sexist nigger in charge of our country."

"How can you call him a nigger?"

"In spite of what you've been taught to believe a nigger is someone who ignorant and our president is definitely a grade A idiot."

"We are in agreeance with him being an idiot but what got you so fired up that you had to get arrested for."

"The executive order that has reinstates Ronald Reagan's Abortion 'Global Gag Rule"

"I'm not into politics. You going to have to explain 'Global Gag Rule' to me like I'm a two year old."

"The global gag rule punishes women in already challenging circumstances by putting life-saving services out of reach. It causes cuts in services, increases in fees, and closures of clinics. In many instances, these are the only providers in remote and poverty stricken communities. Making them more disadvantaged."

"Wow! There is no reason for such a thing but what was his reasoning."

"Claiming to save 600 million tax dollars per year by cutting US funding for international health organizations that offers abortions. But he is just blowing hot air. Helms amendment has prevented US tax dollars from funding overseas abortions since 1973. He just trying to fund that damn wall. Women around the world deserve to make important personal health care decisions without politicians in Washington interfering."

I started half listening Free was going in and out of her Black Panther jargon. Some of it was understandable but other parts was straight rhetoric, boarder line plain gibberish. I could tell from the foam around her mouth she was about to fizz and pop. I hit the gas to 129th street. Free need to let off steam and I didn't want to be around for the smoke. I had twenty minutes to get back to pick Joie up from her first visit with Dom. On the drive downtown my mind wondered what was

Dom telling Joie? What was Joie telling Dom? I've seen different sides of Dom. The craze side is when he has a blank stare in his eyes. I saw it when he beat Lippa face in. He keep slamming his fist into Lippa face. With blood splashing into the air like red raindrops and the sound of bones crushing, hurting my teeth like ice cold water, Dom keep drumming into the bloody putty that once was a human face. When Dom boil with rage he is dangerous. Then its times Dom dance to Mimi's every word like a puppet. Dom has a secret side that I discovered while reading his love letters to Mimi. Who would peg Dom as a sensitive gentleman? I made it back with two minutes to spare. I step out of the car to greet Ms. Nelson and Joie. Joie ran to me with open arms. When she wraps her little arms around my neck and plant her little cold lips on my cheek my mind goes blank and my heart takes over. I wanted to slow feed Dom to Joie with short play dates like forty five minutes in a park or a trip to the zoo or museum. Light before the heavy. The courts are force feeding Dom to Joie three hours at a time. I didn't want to apply any pressure but I wanted to know every single detail. I keep looking through the rearview mirror hoping she just start talking. I was prying and only getting yes and no answers. All I found out was he is friendly, she had fun, they played games. And Ms. Nelson was there the whole time. Home sweet home. Finally I was settled in my condo in front of the window wall in the living room. It's ten pm do you know where your day went? My day started with Katherine squawking demanding voice. Amy's breakdown for the burning body was found in Green Acres Mall. I said a small pray for the victim and family. Running into Ashley with her boo boo kitty haircut, tight cheap business suit and ran down leaning pumps was something I could pass on. She hang around money but didn't come from money and it showed. Her uppity tone in her voice made me want to clip her in the throat but I always display restraints. Then the whole Dom and Joie thing. My mind still has a list of questions. Since when a conversation between a parent and a child is deemed privilege? My head is still pound from Free's Black Panther jargon. I deserved every drop of the glass of wine before I call Chuck's cellphone for the hundredth time today. UGGGGGHHHH! I want to know who is the disrespectful person ringing my doorbell? And Norman doorman is off his job. What happen to the call upstairs, granting access? I swung the door open ready to throw darts with my eyes. But I was to surprise to see Nathan...

Oh my god! Something happened to Chuck? Please don't tell me something happened to Chuck!!

"Did he leave his gun and badge home?"

"You're not going to keep asking questions and you not giving me no answers, WHERE MY HUSBAND?

"I think he went undercover, but I haven't been able to contact him. Right now he's a missing person."

EIGHT

Amy crawls around the exterior of car, she slither into the back seat of Chuck's car. CHUCK, LOOK BEHIND YOU!

I kept dreaming the same part of the dream. I can't sleep. If I fall asleep I see Amy crawling around the exterior of car and I jumped up out of my sleep in a panic. I've been up most of the night, high of coffee. I was shaking with caffeine and fear. Two nights straight, no Chuck. I can feel it in my stomach something horrible has happened. I sat on the edge of the couch with my head in my hands. My head was spinning. Joie woke up and found me downstairs in the living room. I spruce up of the couch, painted a smile on my face and turned on the TV to silence the chaos ringing in my head. Just great, the last thing I needed is to see Ashley's under made up face and that nasal holier than thou voice.

"Good Sunday morning, New York. I'm Ashley Collon filling in for Marc Brooks. It's 7 am and it's 80 degrees outside with lots of sun. Breaking news, Long Island police department has provided an update on the burnt body found in Green Acres Mall's parking garage yesterday morning by parking garage security. The police is releasing camera footage of a car leaving the garage seconds after the other car engulf into flames. The remains are still unidentifiable the police department wants to bring peace to the unsuspecting family. The camera didn't catch an image of the license plates so the police department is looking for the community to provide any information. We going to show the side view of the car one more time. Long Island police department is pleading with the community if anyone see anything or knows anything contact 1-877-TIPS."

If I didn't know any better that looks a lot like Ms. Janet's run downed green '97 Honda Civic. My God, Mimi who have you done? My mind immediately travelled backward to the night in Brentwood. Tears escaped from my eyes. The coldness of the night crept into my bones, the aroma of burning flesh clogged my nose. She's done it again.

"What's wrong?"

Joie's tiny voice of concern bought me back to reality. I explained away my tears with worry for Chuck. I quickly change the subject with an offer of chocolate chip waffles for breakfast.

"My father said Chuck isn't coming back."

"Did he tell you that yesterday?"

"Uhmm, I'm going to miss Chuck but I don't need a pretend daddy anymore cause my real father is here now."

"Did your father tell you where Chuck was going?"

"Yup!"

"Are you going to tell me where Chuck went?"

"My father said good people turn into angels, with wings and everything and live in the clouds. Then there's bad people they catch on fire and burn forever underground. Chuck is a bad man so he is burning underground."

"What makes Chuck a bad person?"

"He wanted to take you away from me, Auntie Mimi and my father and put you in a hospital."

Her words pushed me up against the kitchen island. I put my right hand over my chest to check if my heart was still beating. I'm completely speechless and numb but my tears screamed rage, pain and betrayal. Dom and Mimi has over stepped for the last time. Mimi have turn my life upside down in just thirty days. She got the ball of bullshit rolling with making Dom file for visitation right. Little did I know she was sneaking Joie up to the prison to see him, all a long. Oh no, she didn't stop there she was running around using my identity and credit cards. Rented out a hotel room a thousand dollars a night and I'm not getting into miscellaneous charges for a hundred here, two hundred there. But nothing piss me off more than her inviting herself to Joie's school. It was adding a spit in the face to a stab in the back, I have no idea how many times she made pop-up visits at the school. Dom is an innocent puppet with Mimi's hand up his ass. Dom nor Mimi knows anything about rising child. That's why they left Joie with me in the first place. The two of them had no right to fill Joie's young impressionable head with their alterative facts. Their actions are straight up offensive to the last seven years of my life that I dedicated to Joie. I truly take pride in being a great mother to Joie. Always providing her with the finest. Rising her with everything I missed out on. Her paramount education flowed from adult vocabulary and esteem comprehension. Joie is a strong but delicate flower. I won't allow Mimi to puck her innocents. I've always shown Mimi nothing but respect. Never once have I questioned none of evil plans to destroy lives. She has disrespect me for the last time. I had to confront Mimi. Most importantly I needed to know did she really kill Chuck.

***

I'm angry enough to comfort Mimi but wasn't mentally strong enough to approach Mimi alone. I barely sleep anymore. Every time I close my eye I see that frighten nightmare. All night I've been waiting on Nathan's call. I need to hear news on Chuck. I wish I could just hear his voice. Last night Nathan was talking but not saying anything. I stop calling Chuck phone and started calling Nathan's phone. All I want is five minutes with Chuck. I needed him to know that even though we're going through it, I'll never change my heart, I love him today just as much as I did, when I fell in love with him five years ago. The day is fresh in my mind just like the love in my heart. Amy, Joie and I were living on top of each other in the South Bronx matchbox. I had to be a full time student to honor my scholarship, so I went to school during the day and Amy baby sat Joie. Then at night we switched. Amy worked nights and I stayed with Joie. Thanks to Miss Janet's generosity I was afforded to work on the weekends. Saturday's and Sunday's I work double shifts as, a waitress, a dishwasher, and a housekeeper. In two semesters I've aged at least five years. I started developing joint pain and stiff muscles. I was juggling too much and I have to admit I'm an over achiever, so I had to get straight A's in all my classes, putting in a little more the ordinary employee making myself an extraordinary worker, and being an A plus mom is always number one on my list. Overloaded with responsibility, I was ready to bust at the seams. I finally caught a break. My straight A granted my access to online classes, giving me more time home with Joie. I scored a nice paying job fitting to my schedule. Sandy's flower shop in Manhattan. Working with Sandy wasn't work it was more like flower school. Learning about something I love was a pleasure. One Sunday after a tall handsome man came in the flower shop needing arrangements for a funeral. By looking at him I notice my bird nest hairdo and dirty aprons. His almond shape eyes were red with worry and his gentle manly voice echo with pain. I knew the person who passed is very close to the sexy man. I begin asking question to help him choice his floral arrangements. The more questions I asked the weaker he got. Without warning he broke down. I try my best to soothe his aching heart. He was completely hopeless with grief. Clearly ordering the flowers for his father's funeral wasn't the job for him right then. My heart started hurting for him. I couldn't help myself I felt compel to help him. At that very moment I heard Mimi's words ringing in between my ears "You can't smother everybody." I laughed in my head Mimi was never good at vocabulary, she was saying the word right but was trying to combine two words, mother and smother to describe my ability to look after a person with sympathetic eyes, being protectively with my heart, sometimes disproportionate but always genuine. My behavior was involuntary. I took the weeping man to the diner two blocks over on Second Avenue. We were seated upon entrance. I ordered just coffee and a scone for both of us. I did all the talking about myself hoping he gab on to a word. But he just stared aimlessly into space. I talked about everything under the sun, I had run out of words. The one topic I was trying to avoid was the last thing I had. Unwittingly I just asked about his deceased father. I had his full attention. Memories, words and thoughts slopped out. He went through the seasons of emotions, happy, sad, mad and playful. He babbled his life in pieces and blabbed fragment of his raw self. My heart was eavesdropping and by chance I fell in love. I accidently noticed that he talks with his eyes. His words so authentic made him trustworthy. Randomly I comfort him with a gentle touch. Who would guess I would feel a spark? We parted with a friendly hug. He thanked me. In his mother's eyes he had to be strong for both of them. I allowed him to be hurt without being ashamed. I decided right then if he let me I'll take care of him. I can tell by the way you carry himself, he feel like he was on his own. He hate being alone, he ain't the only one. But I'll be there for him. I took Chuck's father's funeral flowers personal. Not only did I stay up all night setting up the display arrangements but I also was bright eye and bushy tail at the church setting up around the casket. I impressed Sandy along with myself. Chuck entered the church as I was leaving. He was cute in the diner but in his uniform he is downright sexy. He thanked Sandy and myself, and I began to follow Sandy toward the exit. Chuck grab my right hand and said "I know this ain't the traditional date spot but would you staying with me. I don't think I could get through this without you..." My heart sunk down to my feet. Of course I'll stay, it's been five years. He courted me like a true gentleman, dinners, movies and gifts. We instantly were serious. His first encounter with Joie was just too sweet. She took to him and he was automatically in love. He splurge on a queen fitting wedding for us, with Joie the cuties princess flower girl in the world. On my wedding day I was truly getting the real Prince Charming. Chuck is the perfect husband and loving father. I'm ready to have his baby. I love Chuck more than I love my friends. And as much as Mimi thinks she's a savor, only Chuck can say me. He has a past and I have mine. I can't sleep thinking of the lies cause I know the truth is going hurt. I've asked about him and he told me everything. What was I thinking? I can be myself with Chuck! His heart won't change, he would still feel the same. My heart is showering my pillow with tears it's been too long without Chuck. I don't know if I hate Mimi for selling me a dream or myself for buying into it. I can't keep crying hoping things will jut wash back into place. I had to come at Mimi in a unit and do something about her actions. Mimi had my life belly up, I can only imagine what she had done to Free and Tricia. I reached out to Free first. Free first cause I'm hoping she would have my back and help me put Tricia on broad. Free usually has a lot to say about everything but today she just sat in the front passenger seat silent with arms folded across her chest. Baiting her into conversation by asking about her love interest she mentioned before. Everybody likes talking about matters of the heart. But I hit a nerve.

"I literally begged her to keep her out of this. Mimi makes mess out of our lives but she'll never physical hurt any of us. I try to explain to Amy that Mimi manipulates people to her benefit then dispose of them. Bless her heart she can see the good even in evil..."

Once Free mentioned Amy I had to relive my horrible nightmare one more time.

"Sweetie that was no nightmare that was reality. But getting Amy and Dickey involved is putting their own lives at risk. Mimi is a savage. She played with Amy's mind and Dickey's body to get them do what she say. Mimi's game is treacherous. The same way she used Amy's mind in her favor, she can make Amy's mind turn on Amy. And Amy unsuspecting nature don't even see it coming. And poor young Dickey has no idea that having sex with Mimi will get him killed, just ask Lippa how that turned out for him."

Free said a mouthful. I felt like I've been walking around in a bubble. How could I miss all these things happening right under my nose and I didn't smell anything. I don't want to believe Mimi would intentionally hurt me and take Chuck away from me. But I know she is capable of anything. We drove to pick up Tricia. Tricia jumped in the back seat of my car. She didn't have to say a words. I know she was mad by how hard she was popping her gum.

"I'm an adults now. I don't know what y'all going to do but I'm going to reclaim my life. She can't bully me around no more pulling my strings to move the way she wants me to. She's a bitch!"

For once in my life I agree with Tricia self-centered words. Mimi is a bitch. Within minutes of Tricia getting in the car Free's phone started ringing. Free received a call from Kelly, the bartender, Mimi's male friend, Dom, is at 167th street off Jerome Avenue, Mimi is sure to follow. I drove to the bar. With my foot on the gas I was building up a blast for Mimi. Free is blowing smoke from her nose, fuming from Mimi's actions. Tricia just hoped Mimi would still be there when we arrived. When we walked in the bar with strength by unity. Mimi and Dom was playing a game of pool with my credit card holding there tab. Can you believe her boldness? She talked and walked in circles. She was laughing and joking like she was on joy riding thru life. She moved like she was relinquished of all controls. It felt like the emancipation of Mimi. She was strong as rock, free as a bird and as bright as the sun. I kept my eyes to floor. I didn't want to make eye contact with the devil in Jordan's in fear I might turn to stone and lose my nerve to say what I have on my heart. We took turns airing our grievances. Tricia couldn't help herself she shouted her gripes to Mimi's face. The injustice to Amy's mental state made Free slam her fist on the table. The sudden loud sound cause me to jump but Mimi didn't budge. Mimi's nonchalant attitude nudged my nerve and before I could bite my tongue I was screaming out about every act Mimi committed against me. I spoke words that were bottle up inside me still I was a child. I purged all my thoughts of Mimi to her face. With tears and snot rolling down my face, lips and chin, I'm completely exhausted but felt completely refreshed.

"Are y'all done? I hope y'all feel better cause it's my turn. All of you are a bunch of ungrateful bitches! How dare y'all have any fucking complaints! Gege you keep forgetting Joie is my daughter. Why this and why that. Letting you rise her is a privilege! Every fire I ever started was to keep our secret and to keep us together! We belong together. Them greedy bitches, Erica and Nicole and now Chuck. If you feel some kind of way you better shake it off before you say something to me. Cause each and every fire I started each and every one of you was there and didn't stop me which makes you as guilty as me. I wish y'all know how many fires I put out before y'all ass got burnt."

"How do you know Chuck would've accepted the secret? He really loved me. You didn't have to kill him!"

"Technically I didn't kill him! Right Free?"

"Fuck you Mimi, I told you to keep Amy out if your games."

"I knew you always had a thing for me."

"Mimi why Chuck?" I had to know Mimi's reasoning.

"Too be so smart you can be so stupid. Chuck is a fucking cop, the blue blood comes before you. He was going to solve that damn case, instead he died trying. And I know everything he knows from the night I fucked him. You know a wet dick make the mouth spit. He made it last all night. I left my marks on his back. I know you saw it. He's an animal in the bed. And FYI I didn't kill him Amy and Dickey did. I just cleaned up the mess."

Mimi shot words in the air to pierce our hearts. Tears rolled down my cheeks to mourn the people, living and deceased, who lost their life to Mimi. Her vulgar confession made my heart hurt. How could anybody so heartless?

"Stop your fucking crying! I sent Chuck to you to watch him! You fell in love with the target, your fault not mine. You was wrong from the start. No worries nobody will never ID him. I have his gun, badge and wallet."

"Why you keep saying you send Chuck to me? Did you kill his father too?

"I do what's necessary."

"Damn Mimi, take it easy! You know Gege is sensitive." Tricia offered her condolences. Tricia know all too well the feeling of losing someone you truly love to Mimi's bloody hands.

"Gege you know she want us all to herself, love is forbidden and apparently red leather jackets." Tricia fired her words at Mimi.

"Poor little innocent Gege! She's not all that pure. Did you all knew she put a computer chip in my daughter like she's some FUCKING Yokie?"

This is what Mimi does to deflect from her evil doing she point the attention elsewhere. Now I'm under the microscope of judgmental eyes. I will not apologize for being protective over Joie.

"Tricia yes I burned that fucking red jacket right next to Chuck ass and I'll do it again. I call it a BOGO special, burn one, get one. Fuck that leather jacket, I wore it for a few days before I burnt it, if that makes you feel any better? You hold on to the jacket cause it's a reminder of Lippa. Are you going to spend the rest of your life crying over a dead man? Lippa is gone! I did you a favor! You was in love with Lippa but his heart would forever belong to me. Move the fuck on!"

Mimi stabbed and jabbed with her words. Mimi's blade of words carved pain into our hearts making our eyes bleed.

"Damn! Mimi you can put the gloves away!"

"Oh hail, Free the feminist, civil rights leader, the people's champion, the freedom warrior who is a prisoner in her own skin. Cause she has one weakness the world doesn't know about...

Mimi slowly floats over to Free as her vicious words turned soft. She is talking loud enough so we all could hear her. She spoke into Free's ear. Her words at a seductively tone pounding on Free's eardrums.

"You love the scent, feel and taste of a woman. Why are you two petting up Gege? Do she know about y'all love affairs, Free is sleeping with Amy and Tricia is molesting Dickey?"

"I ask you to leave Amy out of this but instead you tricked her into doing you dirty work. Do you plan on playing with her mind like you do to all of us or will you kill her like you did Erica? Why can we have a life outside of you?"

"I'm not asking! Stay away from Dickey before you jealous lapdog hurt him."

"Amy hands been dirty! And I can't make any promise! Dickey is a fun ride. We all have secrets and now that we know each other we can move forward. Never forget my job is to protect one secret and I'm going to do that by any means necessary! Now that y'all done bitching and moaning we have business to discuss. I followed Aileen around all week with damn red jacket on. I think she's finally drove her crazy ass over the edge. Now she see the damn jacket without it even being there. I know Nathan is about to commit her ass to the nut house. No shade Gege. That still leaves Nathan. He is becoming a problem. He only has Chuck's puzzle pieces right now but he's gathering his own pieces. If he fits things together you know what happens to us. So the plan is to follow him tomorrow. We going to do it in shifts so everybody can be seen in their everyday life just in case we need alibies.

Alibies? I immediately started shaking. Mimi's reign wasn't over.

"Officer Miller rises early so me and Dom going is taking the 1st six hours then Free, Gege, than Tricia. No phones! And don't forget this all about us."

NINE

Today is a difficult day. Reality has settle in. After a several days of fighting the truth I had to surrender to the facts. All though the license plate was removed from the car from the pile of chard rubbish a car part serial number was recovered. In black and white the proof that the burnt debris is Chuck's Dodge and what human remains belonged to Chuck. I had fragments of Chuck's notes that needed to be picked through. All I wanted was a day to lay in the bed and wait for it to pass me by. Drinking a pint of Jameson to put me to sleep is waking me up with a twisted stomach aching down to my bones. I reached into the hamper pool of stale clothing swimming with the scent of sweat. And by luck of the draw I pulled a pair of black slack and a striped button up shirt. The black slacks needed a little cold water to rinse out the pizza sauce from last Thursday's dinner. I sprayed deodorant on the underarms of the striped button up shirt before hitting up my armpits. Tossed on the now dry slacks. Loafs on my feet no socks. Splashed some water on my face and rinsed my teeth out with capful of mouthwash and walked out toward the door. The air in my bachelor studio apartment is a toxic mix. My head is tripping and my head is spinning from the scent. Both my mind and insides are formulating gas. The coffee table sitting on top of the area rug is decorated with dinner remains. The stench of old sausage and pepperoni is coming from the pizza box with half eaten slice from last Thursday's dinner. The white Chinese food container with chicken bones stink of leftovers from Wednesday. A clear clam shell container whiff from the scraps of fish taco Tuesday. Snippets of half eaten French fries, potato chips crumbs and empty beer cans seasoned the living room area rug. Before locking the door I leave behind a spray of some air fresher to clear the congested air that I looked, felt and smelled like last week. I stopped off at Kooke Kornell mental institution to check up on Aileen. Her super simply thinking caused her to attack a woman just because the woman was wearing a red leather jacket. The death of her only son has driven her completely out of her mind, now she's parked in hospital instead of jail. She gave the poor woman fifty seven stiches in total with a broken glass bottle. I had to stop by to see how she make it through her 1st off many nights in the hospital. She babbled on and on about a fictions conversation with "Tricia". It was breaking my heart to see my strong sister be so weak. As much as I wanted to be by her side I couldn't stand to see that side of her. I drove to the station with a heavy head and a hefty heart. Chuck was on to something. Did the death of the two teenage girls and Lippa's death have the same killer? How does Dom fit in? And what did Chuck find out that might have cost him his life. Technically Chuck was "missing." Captain said we couldn't deem Chuck dead cause we didn't have a body but I know he was gone, I could feel it in my heart. No body no case. My hands were tied on the legal side. So, I called Ashley and asked her to use her reporter connection to get any information on

Gemini Patricia Freeman. I could feel it in my bones Gemini is in the middle. I needed the case file for the two girls. So I stop by Chuck's condo. To my surprise Gege was very helpful and very concerned. But behind her eyes I could see she knew more than she was saying. It was so awkward being in her space. Her ora wasn't the same. She talked different. She walked differently. Even Joie was acting different, something is off. She is definitely hiding something. For some strange reason my sister's voice was ringing in my head... "The aunt Janet's apartment is on 105th street between second and third avenue." I went back to the station and see what information was gathered on the possible witness that was driving a green '97 Honda Civic from the burnt body in the garage case. I have a hunch that's the burnt remains is Chuck body. There were 150 registered green '97 Honda Civic in NYC. Fine police work has cut the list down to the last ten in 3 hours. My eyes almost fell out of my head when I saw Janet Lloyd name residing at 146 east 105th street, apt # 2c. I couldn't get there fast enough. I walked up to the 2nd floor of the building sitting in the middle of the block. I knocked on apartment 2C. The stout 87 year old woman answered the door. She held her torn housecoat together with her left hand. She had a head full of pink rollers and orange framed reading glass hanging on to her nose.

"Good morning, I'm Detective Nathan Miller and this is Detective Melina Winger and we're looking for Ms. Janet Lloyd." I had to bring a fellow female blue to contact a female civilian, for comfortably and precaution. Winger is just that, a wing along for the ride. Ms. Lloyd invited us in with her comfy tone, she did some quick last minute tidying to create seating for Winger and myself on the floral printed three seater. Her organized cluttered home is relaxing. Her elderly mannerism forced her to offer us tea and cake. We both declined even though the offer is very tempting.

"That me, how can I help you?" The pleasant 87 year old woman spoke gently, grandmotherly warmth.

"Do you still own green '97 Honda Civic?"

"No sir, I haven't driven a car in years. For years it was sitting in the parking garage on 99th street, costing me a hundred dollars a month. Then seven years ago I sold it to a lovely young woman named Amy."

"Do know Amy's last name?"

"It's Castillo like the Spanish singing Alberto Castillo"

"How did you meet "Amy"?"

"She's a friend of a friend."

"Well. Did you know Amy never change the name on the car?"

"No I didn't, she must've forgotten."

"Before you sold the car did you loan the car to anyone one?"

"Oh yes, about eight years ago I let the neighbor's daughter use it. It came in handy to a teenager in New York City. I wasn't using it. Everything I need is in a three block radius."

"Does the neighbor still live here?"

"The father, Taurus Freedman, still lives here but the daughter been gone. They use to live down the block but after had a big fire the move here. The poor woman died in the fire. Rumor has it the daughter set the fire. But nonetheless neither recovered from the loss of their property, mother and wife. Don't waste your time knocking he's a mailman. He starts his day at 5:30 am and whatever energy he has left after a hard day of work he drinks away at Jojo's bar down the street."

"What do you know about the daughter?"

"Well there were a few of them... there's my favorite Free. She has the brain of a panther, heart and roar of a lion. She love civil rights movies. We would stay up all night just embracing our culture. Oh, I could never forget about the fashion model miss Tricia, honey. She change clothes hundred times a day. She loves fabric, designs and belts. She would sit on the floor for hours looking at clothes in fashion magazines to shopping catalogs. Clothes is that child's life. Back in my day I was a Las Vegas show girl. I walked away with some of the costumes. Tricia loved playing in the sequined fabric. Her face would light up like a Christmas tree. Then there's Gege. She's so sweet it'll make you teeth hurt. She would help me around the house. Go to the store for me. Sometimes she would even cook for me. I enjoyed her company. She's very intelligent. I went with her to two attendance and honor roll award ceremonies in her honor. She's the daughter I wish I had. Unfortunately I never bared any children. None the least I had Gege. A child with a heart of gold, my precious angel. Then there's the monster, more like the devil, Mimi. Dark, scary and plain rude, just no couth. She set my cat on fire cause I didn't let her borrow the car on a school night. That one is just an evil thing. If I see her coming I cross the street, she makes my skin crawl."

"But I thought you said there was only one daughter. I'm completely confessed. You listed four different names."

"Yes that right."

"But you just described four different girls."

"They are all one in the same."

"What does that mean?"

"Each one of them is defined in personality and style, all four of them are completely different people, even their voices sound different but all sharing one body."

The information dropped on me by Ms. Lloyd made my brain itchy and scratchy. The elderly woman is too honest to make up such a story. I believed her. Gemini is more than one person? How could Gemini fool so many people for so long? My next stop is her father's job. He works at the 34th street post office. I'm sure her father had to notice something. It would've been courteous to hold a light conversation with Winger during the drive downtown but my mind is twisted. I had this overwhelming feel Chuck stubbed onto this information and lost his life. I made a promise to protect my partner with my life and that what im going to do.

"Excuse me Mr. Freeman?"

"Who's asking?"

"I'm Detective Nathan Miller and this is Detective Melina Winger."

"How can I help you?"

"We want to ask you some questions about your daughter."

"Is she ok?"

"She's fine just trying to understand some things."

"Well I can't help you. I haven't seen her since she showed up at my door with a baby in her arms, she wouldn't tell me where she got the baby from. Said she's doing a favor for friend. What kind of friend drops a baby on a teenager? I told her to give that baby back or don't come back! She made her choice when she didn't come back."

"So it's not her baby?"

"No sir! I seen that girl every day I would've notice if she was pregnant. I have a drink now and then but I ain't blind."

"Do you know about Mimi, Free and Tricia?"

"Mimi is a name I haven't heard in a while. Every time Gege was caught doing something wrong she put the blame on "Mimi." Her mother use to entertain "invisible" friends. I didn't partake or condone it."

"How about Free and Tricia?"

"No never heard of them. I hope you got all that you need I have work to do."

"Did your daughter ever talk to somebody, like a professional about Mimi?"

"Yes she spent six month under the care of a psychiatrists, named Tia Lovell after the fire."

"Fire?"

"Yes, my wife died in that damn fire. I lost my whole live in a split of a second. My heart hasn't healed yet. And the only thing Gege had to offer was placing the blamed Mimi. The system wanted to put her in jail but my brother's wife is a lawyer, she got Gege into a hospital to get her the help she needed, but when she was released I think she was worst then before. But I'm no doctor."

"Thank you for your time sir."

Looking into Mr. Freeman's eyes I saw the brokenness. His sense of feeling the past that moment vanished in the smoke of that fire. My heart ached for him. The more I dig the deeper it gets. The Gege I've known for the last 5 years wasn't capable of setting a fire resulting in death. She's the gentlest loving being. I know the Doctor wasn't going to tell what I wanted to know but she could give me something. Dr. Lovell had her over high end private practice on 5th Avenue. She made us wait 45 minutes before letting us into her office. A model figure with wild coral hair stood on 6 inch pumps. Open the door to the office inviting us in. Her red lipstick told she meant business. She took a seat in her high back chair behind her desk with her hand folded holding up her chin.

"I can't be much use to you. I will never doctor patient code."

"We not asking to do that. When she was in the hospital and you was treating her she had to make a friend or two. Can you tell us who the friend is?"

"Yes, she did make a friend, Amy Castillo. That's it. Detectives, you two have to go I have session in fifteen minutes."

I returned to the precinct and took up the space of an integration room. I lay down all the facts. Domonique Thomas is the convicted murder of my nephew Lippa. The two burnt teenager last since with "Tricia." According to my sister "Tricia" had influence on Lippa's death. The picture of the shooter outside of my sister's apartment building. Could all 3 incidents involve the same person? My mind rewind to the party years ago when my sister attacked Gege calling her Tricia. Was she just acting crazy or was she on to something? Domonique Thomas's tattoo and Ms. Lloyd collaborate that Mimi, Free, Tricia and Gege are one person. I don't want to believe I committed my sister into the hospital and she was right all along, I have to figure this thing out. Domonique Thomas and

Gemini Patricia Freeman are connect through the birth certificate. I'm looking at all the pieces the burnt teenagers, Lippa's crushed face, the female shooter in the red leather jacket and possibly Chuck's body burnt to death in the parking garage. I printed out the image of the car leaving the garage moment after the car went up in flames. By chance Amy Castillo owners a forest green 97' Honda civic but legally it registered to Ms. Janet Lloyd. Amy Castillo just happens to be an employee at Gege's flower shop. I know it means something that they have been friends for years. A friendship that ignited in a mental hospital. I know the answer with proof is staring at me but I just couldn't see it. Ashley called me to meet her at Larry's on 200TH and Hollis, way out in Queens. Larry's is a known police beer and burger hangout spot. I spotted Ashley sitting in the back. She waved her right hand in the air beckoning me to come over to her. Ashley was talking so fast she was foaming at the mouth and stuttering. She wanted to take Gege down so bad she could taste it.

"Gemini Patricia Freeman's mother, Stacey Freeman, died in a fire when she was 13 years old. In the police notes, they knew she set the fire but couldn't prove it. Due to lack of evidence she escape jail by being committed in the mental hospital for 6 months. After her release she was arrested 15 times with 15 different mug shots. 5 arrest at "Tricia" for shoplifting in clothing stores, 7 arrest as "Free" disturbing the peace, disorderly conduct, and assault on an officer. 3 arrest as "Mimi", the fire bug, for setting fire to neighborhood pets."

I stare down at the 15 photos and couldn't accept the truth looking me in the eye. Looking with a naked eye, without absolute doubt it appears to be 4 separate people. But if you look deeper it definitely is Gege in all 15 photos. It felt like the room was closing in on me. I started sweating and my throat started closing. I had to go outside from some air my stomach is bubbling.

***

My heart is ponding. My hands are so sweaty they are slipping off the starring wheel. Nathan knows everything. We followed him to a restaurant named Larry's on 200ᵀᴴ and Hollis in Queens.

"See we been following him all day while he retrace our steps from the past. I promise he's the last one! Our secret is in his hands and our hand will end up in cuffs."

Mimi answer to everything is death. But we didn't have time on our side. Any minute he will piece everything together, if hasn't already. Out of nowhere he walks outside the restaurant and walks over to the driver side of his car.

"RUN HIM OVER!" Mimi shouts into my ear from the back seat. Her words came with a heavy tap on my shoulder.

"DON'T DO IT!" Free wants an end to violence.

"DO IT NOW!" Mimi screams into my brain as she slap my shoulder.

All the yelling and touching had me confessed. I closed my eyes and instantly was standing in the middle of icy white walls. The frosty panic of being in complete isolated took my breath away. I shake my head from side to side, hoping my view is just a figment of my imagination. The everlasting gray skies of segregation hovering over my head. I take a deep breath and inhale the overpowering aroma of redundant amounts of bleach failing to conceal the whiff of blood, feces and urine. The anxiety of my mind's surroundings fueled the strength of my mind. I closed my eyes and started punching and pounding with my fist to be released from the white wall prison. When I opened my eyes I was seating back in my car. I noticed I've pummeled my fist bloody on the staring wheel. With tears in my eyes, I set my vision on Nathan. I'm determined not to relive my past. I just can't handle the horror again. I'm staring at Nathan leaning into the driver's side window of his car.

"DO IT NOW!" Mimi screams directly into my ear drum making my heart beat loud enough for me to hear it. I didn't want to but I had to. I closed my eyes extra tight, squeezed the steering wheel with both of my bloody hands and pressed my foot down hard on the gas. I stared crying when I felt the car roll over a large bump.

***

Good evening, New York. I'm Ashley Collon reporting live with breaking news. The police department is asking the public for help three separate crimes were committed but all connected. Just moments ago a police detective was just run down by this green '97 Honda Civic. The officer is at the hospital in critical condition. The suspect abandon the green '97 Honda Civic a block away from the crime scene. Officers on the scene say this green '97 Honda Civic can possibly be the same car on the surveillance video involved in another open case. The burning body found in Green Acres Mall's parking garage, just days ago. The scorched remains are still unidentified. Weeks ago police released this footage of the shooter in another open case. In the footage there is a female wearing a ski mask, red leather jacket, black pants and black sneakers shooting into an apartment window near Patterson public housing. The bullets went through the window piecing victim, Aileen Miller's leg. All three crimes are linked. The police department is pleading with the community if anyone see anything or knows anything please contact 1-877-TIPS. I'm Ashley Collon handing back to the studio."

If you or someone you know needs assistants:

National Alliance on Mental Illness (NAMI) 24/7 *Helpline*: 1-800-950-NAMI (6264).

www.ingramcontent.com/pod-product-compliance
Lightning Source LLC
Chambersburg PA
CBHW070340260626
47160CB00003B/1101